Birds of Britain

ABOVE A Great Tit displays its colourful plumage.

PREVIOUS PAGES The Spoonbill, immediately
recognizable from its extraordinary, long, spoon-
shaped bill. It may be seen in spring and
summer on some east and south coast estuaries.

OVERLEAF An adult Mistle Thrush with a large,
grown family. The site of this nest is typical, an
open situation on the branch of a tree. This species
is also known as the Storm Cock because of its habit
of singing in wild and windy weather.

OPPOSITE CONTENTS The Little Owl is an
introduced species that at first thrived and is now
less numerous. Only 8 in. (200 mm) high, it is able
to catch birds as big as Blackbirds.

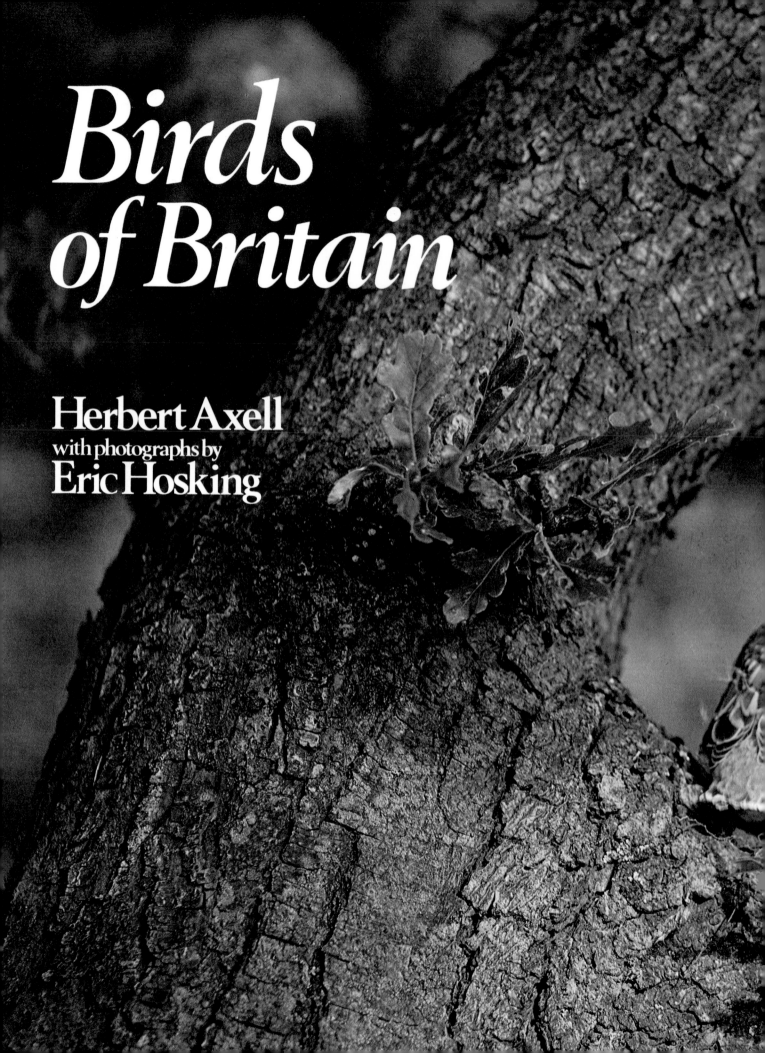

Birds
of Britain

Herbert Axell
with photographs by
Eric Hosking

Artus

Contents

1 The Life of Birds

Of all the kinds of wildlife that enrich our world, birds give the most pleasure to most people. Their immense variety of colour, shape and behaviour is there for all to see, to be taken for granted and vaguely enjoyed, or to be wondered at and keenly appreciated by the more thoughtful. Birds are almost everywhere, some even occasionally visit the North Pole, and it is estimated that there may be as many as a hundred thousand million of them.

To the envy of Man, they can fly under their own power. Some can even 'fly' under water. According to their kind, they can perform most of the physical actions that we can; they can walk and run and sing and dance, some better than us, some worse. But, unlike humans, they cannot consciously plan what they are going to do and they have no conscience. Their behaviour is not affected by moral values and they have no emotions of pride or guilt about their responses to instinct. If they need to, or if simply given the chance, they will steal another's food or nest material or mate. But murder and the causing of serious injury within their own species are rare, though in times of extreme food scarcity some birds of prey may eat their dead or weakest nestlings or feed them to stronger young.

From the time a bird begins to peck its way out of the egg, its life is one of constant and mechanical response to innate urges. This response may be improved, more in some species than others, by learning from experience. Its survival will depend on quick response to inherited sensations of fear and aggression; it must forever be alert to possible danger, and the need to escape.

To human eyes it appears that a bird is a machine whose actions are uncalculated and entirely designed for the survival of its own species. In love and conflict its immediate display of emotion is evident in the way it moves its body, limbs, feathers, and beak and the way it uses its voice. A thrush, standing by its nest full of healthy young which it has just fed, does not show its pride and pleasure, if it feels any. Its devoted watching of the brood is simply to make sure it does not miss the emergence of a chick's dropping, so that it can take it away, or swallow it, as a necessary act of nest sanitation. The Swallow, after a long breeding season and just before setting off on a 5,000-mile (8046-km) journey to winter quarters in South Africa, sings with apparent joy as, for the last few times on a golden September day, it flies around the cottage where it nested. We could well believe the bird is happy, possibly at the prospect of a winter under sunny, insect-rich skies. Perhaps it does feel happy, but in fact it may only be letting off steam in response to an excessive production of hormones at this time of year. The shorter days are like those of the spring, when it was required to sing a great deal, while the ending of the breeding season means that the bird's body is under less strain.

Although a bird is not just instinctive, but has a high ability to refine its behaviour, its year is governed entirely by a rhythm of biological events which cause it to mate, moult and, in many species, migrate. Its 'internal clock' tells the time and date by the sun, and causes it to take vitally important actions at the right time. Thus the Cuckoo, wintering in tropical Africa, automatically feels the approach of spring which allows it to begin its long journey northwards. The longer days having apparently stimulated the pituitary and thyroid glands, the sexual organs begin to enlarge and fuel for the trip is stored as fat to be burnt *en route*. At a time varying according to the species and its destination, millions of other migrants of many kinds find themselves becoming restless. A large number will make the journey in nightly stages. One fine evening of settled weather, when the position of the sun or the stars has indicated the right time and direction, the journey is begun.

Depending on the weather, a small bird will travel at about 30 miles (50 km) an hour, its ground speed being much faster downwind at heights of up to 5,000 ft (1500 m). In certain conditions it may fly even higher. It will cover a few or several hundred miles in a night, continuing in daylight if it finds itself over alien territory like the sea or a barren desert. Unconsciously it uses the stars as direction indicators and automatically corrects for drift by flying crabwise or getting back on course on the next leg of its journey. Eventually it reaches its destined breeding area. If it is an adult bird, it will find itself close to where it bred in the previous season, a final exact position being found by local landmarks. A bird in its first year will find itself in a suitable habitat but it must establish a territory not already claimed by an older bird of its own kind. It will, however, be near to having reached the most important stage of its existence, which is to survive the first year of its life. So many dangers threaten the juvenile bird while it is learning to put a keen edge to its inherited abilities that the average life of small birds is not more than eighteen months. Those that survive their first year, however, may live another five or more. Larger birds generally live longer – terns and gulls, ringed in this country as chicks, have lived for over twenty-five years.

In the case of most migrant land birds, the male will be the first to arrive at the breeding quarters so that before the female appears he will have claimed as much territory as he needs and can hold against competitors of his own species. This he does by singing from as many song-posts as can be conveniently found around the edge of the territory he wants. He may also put on an aggressive display, showing a rival who tries to enter that territory the brightest part of his spring plumage, and he may also fight, though rarely to cause serious injury. When the females arrive, the male's

White-fronted Geese arriving from Greenland to spend the winter in Ireland and West Scotland. The V-formation in which they are flying is a highly efficient method of travel adopted by these birds. The leading birds create air eddies which give a lift to the birds behind so aiding their flight. The leading bird, who has the hardest task, eventually drops back and is replaced by a bird from behind.

LEFT The devotion apparent on the face of this Song Thrush, who has just fed her large young, is in fact careful attention to ensure that she does not miss the emergence of a chick's dropping which she will remove or eat immediately as part of the nest sanitation. The hawthorn bush is a common site for such a nest but the mud lining is an unusual feature for nests of British birds.

PREVIOUS PAGES A vividly coloured male Golden Oriole pushes a caterpillar into the wide-open gape of one of its young. This bird is one of the rarest species to breed in this country. Its presence is more often known from hearing its fluty song than from actually seeing it.

A pair of Fulmars engaged in the ritual of courtship display which brings the birds into the right condition for breeding. Fulmars have been increasing in number dramatically and are among the most common of British sea birds. It is a 'tube-nosed' species with nostrils which can be clearly seen on top of the beak.

song and bright plumage play their second vital role in attracting one of them. At first the male shows the same aggression towards his mate-to-be as he would to another male, but gradually, because she does not retreat from his display and behaves in a different way from him, she is accepted. Her own acceptance of the male is strengthened by his continued song and other courtship activity and the fact that his territory is suitable. Song and display by both male and female finally decide the pair bond and are used by the birds well into the breeding season to reassure each other and keep the partnership going.

The birds are brought into the right condition for breeding by a courtship ritual which is different for each species. In many small song birds it is relatively simple, the male perching before his mate with head raised back, wings and tail quivering and spread to display the colourful patches they may have. Courtship feeding is common to many species. At its simplest, in the case of a Robin for instance, the male frequently presents beakfuls of caterpillars and adult insects to his mate who accepts them with the crouching, quivering posture of a fledgling asking for food. A larger species, a Marsh Harrier for example, will perform remarkable aerial movements to court his mate, transferring food, a small mammal or a bird, which he has caught, in mid-air to the female who takes it direct from his claws or catches it when he lets it go. A male tern comes into the ternery calling loudly, with a small fish dangling in his bill. He is joined by his mate who follows him very closely and together, in a very lively manner, they slash through the crowded air of the colony. Landing at a special display area, in the case of some species, the male struts around with head held high on outstretched neck, wings drooping, while his mate adopts the food-begging attitude of a hungry youngster.

In some species, like Black Grouse, Ruffs and Avocets, communal display by several males at once is necessary to excite a peak of breeding condition. By the time this state is achieved, the gonads (reproductive glands) of both sexes have enlarged enormously from the tiny, inactive organs they were in the non-breeding season when the carrying of extra weight in the body would have been uneconomic. The male's pair of testes, swollen to hundreds of times the size they were in winter, lie near the kidneys, and from each a sperm duct leads to just within the lip of the cloaca (excretory passage). In the female, which has one active ovary on the left, some of the ova (eggs) swell to contain large yolks, and when fully ripened an ovum enters the funnel entrance of the oviduct which connects, near the opening, with the cloaca, in size and appearance like the male's.

Very few male birds, except in the duck family, have a penis, and mating comes about through the joining of the cloacae, the surrounding ring of feathers and lip of each bird's cloaca being turned outward while the tails are displaced to one side. Many acts of copulation are necessary before a full clutch of ova is fertilized. In most birds the mating occurs on the ground or on a branch; in the case of ducks it is accomplished in the water with the female submerged. Swifts can copulate on the wing. After fertilization, an egg yolk, on its course down the female's reproductive tract, receives the albumen, outer membranes and then the calcified, porous coating which becomes the shell. Colourful pigment is not wasted on the shells of hole-nesting birds whose eggs are hidden, but those which have to survive in the open, as in the case of waders and sea birds, are marked with camouflaging spots and scribbles. The number of eggs in a clutch is fairly constant within each species although those birds which breed in the extreme north of their range tend to lay more than those of their species which breed in the warmer south. The 'egg-shape' is more definite and more necessary in the case of those eggs which are laid in an exposed position: the single, sharply pointed Guillemot's egg is less likely to roll off a narrow cliff ledge and the four large eggs of waders like Ringed Plovers fit together neatly with their narrow ends inwards so that they can all be covered by the small, brooding bird.

The female begins building as a result of the presence of

The Egyptian Goose, a bird which has been introduced to Britain and now breeds wild, is one of the species of wildfowl that mate on the water.

eggs forming within her. In British species nests may vary from the delicate ball of moss, painstakingly woven by a pair of Long-tailed Tits within the shelter of a bramble or thorn bush, to the few pieces of handily available dead plants hastily drawn together on the beach by a pair of terns. Green Woodpeckers may spend days chiselling out a hole in a tree; Starlings, Nuthatches or tits may nest in the hole the woodpecker made last year. Many species of sea birds, living in tenements on safe, sea-cliff ledges, need little or no nest at all. Some, like Little Terns whose eggs resemble the stones among which they are laid on the beach, would be more obvious to predators if surrounded by nesting material. Each species has to provide a home for its eggs according to inherited methods which have allowed the birds to survive. A male Wren will have been urged to build several nests, his mate choosing one and lining it as the development of fertilized eggs occurs in her oviduct. Many species, like Swallows, share the nest-building; in some, for example, Linnets and other finches, the female does all the work, accompanied by the male for protection and encouragement. Migrant birds nest at the same site used in a previous season, or as near to it as may be practicable.

The construction and size of the nest depend on the total bulk of the clutch of eggs and the size of the bird sitting on them, and to its siting. The dozen or so eggs of a Blue Tit, a small bird, require the safety and stability of holes in trees or walls; doves, with only two small eggs, manage with a platform of twigs; Reed Warblers, with five or six eggs, need deep, cup-shaped nests to prevent their eggs falling out when strong winds bend the reeds round which their nests are woven. The kind of nest which is built, or simply chosen, and its site will also depend very much on whether the young will be blind, naked and helpless (altricial) when hatched. Such birds are called 'nidicolous', or in need of the protection of the nest in which they must remain for a long period before they can fly. Those young which are hatched open-eyed and covered with protective down (precocial) are called 'nidifugous', and normally they can leave the nest a few hours after hatching. Following their parents, precocial young can find their own food and can be brooded to protect them from bad weather in the open. Chicks of this kind will have spent a longer time in the shell of larger eggs, to be much better equipped to meet the world when, using their 'egg tooth', a hard nail on the tip of their upper mandible (beak), they peck their way out into it. A Ringed Plover's eggs, for example, are incubated for about twenty-five days and the chicks leave the nest-scrape on the ground very soon after hatching. A Blackbird, of about the same size, incubates its eggs (sits on them to hatch them) for about thirteen days and the nestlings are unable to leave the nest for about another two weeks.

A clutch of Little Tern eggs on the shore is well camouflaged by its pebble-like appearance. Laid on the beaches, these eggs are often trodden on or disturbed by human visitors to the coast and as a result they have become one of the rarest coastal breeding species.

12

The speed of development of the chicks or nestlings is greatly affected by the size of the food supply which, of course, is much affected by the weather. Cold and wet conditions also reduce the time in which nidifugous chicks can spend in looking for food; Avocets, for example, which are early breeders, may take as long as six weeks to fledge in cold springs when they will have to have been brooded for long periods, whereas if they happen to have been hatched from late clutches, in June, the period between hatching and fledging may be as little as four weeks.

The nidicolous young of passerine (perching) species are in close competition with each other when a parent arrives at the nest with food. Except for one young bird which may temporarily be so full of food that it cannot raise its head, the brood demands to be fed by raising quivering, wide-open beaks. Their mouths are generally their most colourful parts at this time of their lives and many species also have bright spots, or small lumps, on their palates which further spur on the parent to feed them. Many kinds of young make their demands stronger with a chorus of cheeping which begins as soon as the approach of an adult is felt, heard or seen. Some larger species, like gulls and herons, encourage their parents to feed them by biting aggressively on their beaks until they cast up a steaming mass of partly digested food from their stomachs. To avoid having this food snatched away by a brother or sister, a chick swallows it as fast as it can, trusting in its parent completely as to the food's suitability. Later in life, on its own, the young bird will be guided by instinct as to what is or is not suitable for its species to eat, but it will have learnt considerably from its parents and will have made many mistakes before experience has taught it to recognize and snatch up food before it is taken by a competitor. Many species, especially gulls, Starlings and crows, are almost omnivorous (that is, they will eat all kinds of food), and in a world crowded with wasteful humans the discovery of food is less of a problem than it is for specialist feeders. Insectivores, like Swifts who must catch their food on the wing, may go for longs periods without food in persistent rainy weather; fish-catching birds, like herons and Kingfishers, may starve if ponds and streams remain frozen for some days as indeed happened in Britain's bitter winter of 1962–3 when thousands of our water birds died. One of the virtues of our very variable climate, however, is that populations may quite quickly recover after many of their number have been destroyed by periods of severe weather. Many of our smaller birds, especially those that do not migrate, have two broods in a year, some three or even four in long warm summers. Food supply, as affected by weather, is a main natural controller of bird populations. The natural economy does not permit a species to be highly successful year after year, and a balance

These beautiful Golden Plover chicks are just hatching. They are 'nidifugous' which means that they are born well developed and, as soon as their down is dry, are able to leave the nest to feed themselves under the watchful eye of their parents.

between the numbers of each kind of bird and the food available to them in the world is roughly maintained by the fact that about four-fifths of the eggs laid do not become flying young.

So that the food available may be distributed fairly among all the birds, different species have had to choose their food very carefully. Many have a very narrow range of diet which requires highly specialized beaks; in Britain they range from the pine-cone-splitting scissors of the Crossbill to the sensitively tipped, deep-probing long bill of the Curlew to the small bill but enormously wide bristle-sided gape of the moth-catching Nightjar. No birds have teeth which would require a heavy jaw and muscles far forward of their centre of gravity. Instead, food is ground in a gizzard located near the middle of the body. Many species, including seed-eaters and others which do not need to feed continuously on small insects, store food in a crop situated on the side of the oesophagus (gullet). Digestion in birds is very rapid and in order to maintain their high metabolism (the swift rate at which food is used up by the body) large quantities are eaten. According to the species and the calorific value of the food to which it is accustomed, a bird's daily intake may be the equivalent of between half and the whole of its own body weight.

The strenuous activity of feeding itself and one or more broods during the breeding season causes a great deal of wear of the bird's plumage and the production of new feathers to maintain its very high body temperature and its flying skills is the next vital phase in its annual cycle. The moult may begin before it has finished caring for its young and is achieved in a variety of ways in the different species or families of birds. Our Northern Hemisphere ducks moult early into an intermediate 'eclipse' plumage and in doing so lose most of their flight feathers at once, so that they have to spend a period of feeding and hiding quietly. Many males, especially of our migrant passerines and waders, do not waste their resources on keeping gaudy feathers outside the breeding season and grow duller plumage for the winter. Swallows and other birds that feed on plankton in the air replace balanced pairs of feathers one at a time so that the way they fly is not affected. Some migrant warblers have only a little time after the breeding season before their departure for Africa, and delay the moult of their important flight feathers and tails until their safe arrival there.

Most adult birds have at least one complete moult annually. A young bird, from the stage when it is a non-flying chick to its first breeding season, undergoes several stages of moult. The down which is present on a bird when it hatches, thick from the start in precocial birds but barely present and patchy in altricial species, is replaced by juvenile plumage before the bird begins to fly. Most small

This Marsh Tit is making use of a nest box which has been thoughtfully erected in a garden. The bird can be sure of finding ample food here. Despite its name, the Marsh Tit does not require a marshy environment.

birds grow the adult plumage they will need for the mating season in two stages before the next spring, but some of our larger birds, most noticeably in the case of gulls, take three to five years before their plumage is completely like that of their parents.

For many small birds, the moult occurs mainly from late July to late August. They need to be quiet and only just active enough to feed themselves and stay out of danger in this period of great demand upon their energy. This, therefore, is the time when we see least of them. Those which have not mated for life, and they are the big majority, have now become freed from their pair bond; their gonads are shrinking into tiny inert organs and they are now almost sexless.

Sedentary birds (those which do not migrate) will have ensured that their young have moved away from their territory so that they are not faced with extra competition for food. Those about to migrate quickly build up fat as fuel for the journey which is about to take place into winter quarters. This may be only within the country, as in the case of Bearded Tits, or a moderate distance away – to Spain, as in the case of some warblers, and the young of our Goldfinches and Linnets, or as far as the very southernmost part of South Africa where our British Swallows go.

A Garden Warbler feeds its hungry brood. The chicks will receive chiefly insects. This nest site is typical in that it provides thick cover for this secretive bird.

15

2 The
Origin of

Birds

*B*irds are the only animals that grow feathers. They have existed for more than 150 million years, since the age of the Dinosaurs in the Jurassic period. Some of the birds found as fossils in rocks from the Eocene epoch of forty to seventy million years ago had already begun to look like those we see today.

Man is much younger, a relatively new animal. His prime ancestor, Ramapithacus, had emerged by some fourteen million years ago and was a small, partially upright ape with man-like teeth. From him evolved the first tool-user whom palaeontologists (those who study fossils) discovered as a member of Man's own family, *Homo*, and who developed, some one and a half million years ago, into our immediate ancestor *Homo erectus*. Our own species, *Homo sapiens*, has existed for only 250,000 years.

Fossil skeletons show that birds evolved from small reptiles. Their relation to Pterodactyls, the reptiles which were flying on wings of skin at a time when birds were developing their own skill, is not possible as each has very different limb structure. Although there is very little direct fossil evidence, it has been proposed that, because of certain apparent skeletal similarities, the most likely ancestors of birds were the crow-sized reptiles Pseudosuchia, members of the Thecodont ('teeth-in-sockets') group that could run on their hind legs and lived about 225 million years ago.

The most conclusive evidence for birds' origin came only in the last century, by dramatic coincidence just two years after Charles Darwin had published his controversial *Origin of Species*. In 1861, the fossil of a reptile/bird, later to be given the now famous name of *Archaeopteryx* ('ancient wing') was found in a quarry near Solnhofen in Bavaria. Another was discovered in 1877 only 10 miles (16 km) away, both specimens having been embedded in limestone which had been silt in a warm coral sea about 150 million years ago. Part of a third specimen was found in 1956, only some 800 yards (250 m) away from the first.

The fossils were of an animal with the skeleton of a reptile, having a long backbone, jaws with teeth, fingers with claws and a long, flexible tail with twenty free vertebrae. But impressions in the rock showed that it also had feathers on the body and longer ones sprouting from the sides of the tail and from the forearms. The structure of the feathers and their arrangement, with the primary flight feathers coming from the hand and the secondaries coming from the ulna (the inner bone in the forearm), were as they are in today's birds. The tail, however, was very different: modern birds' tail feathers sprout from a 'parson's nose', a muscular extension from the pygostyle, the fused ends of the original vertebral column.

Archaeopteryx was about the size and shape of a Magpie, a strange creature in being part-reptile and part-bird. But

PREVIOUS PAGES A drawing from a fossil remains of the first known flying bird which, it has been discovered, lived 150 million years ago. The *Archaeopteryx*, an early ancestor of modern birds, was probably a poor flyer and used claws and fingers, remnants of its reptile ancestry, for climbing trees, from which it was able to glide.

18

because it had feathers it was indeed a bird. This earliest known representative of the class *Aves*, with three long, clawed fingers extending from the bend of the wing, evidently still needed the ability to climb. Its flying, apparently, was limited to little more than gliding; the wings were short and rounded, the skeleton did not contain air cavities for lightness, and the breast bones included no broad-sided keel which would have supported the big pectoral (chest) muscles needed for powerful flight. It probably took another ten million years for birds to develop true, powered flight.

Other fossils have been discovered of forms of birds which had developed in later eras and represent a total of nearly eight hundred species. The number of these fossils which have come to light so far is, however, small; their bones, containing air cavities, are fragile and easily disintegrated, especially in the case of those that lived in forests, and their feathers have been eaten by insects. Skeletal remains from the Cretaceous period of 70 to 135 million years ago, after the time of the *Archaeopteryx*, include those of true birds. These were mostly sea-going species like the 8-in. (200-mm)-high fish-eating tern *Ichthyornis* and the 6-ft 6-in. (2-m)-long *Hesperornis*, an expert swimmer but flightless. The many more and varied fossils from the following epochs showed how birds had made the best possible use of their flying abilities and, developing different forms, had spread over the world to occupy almost every kind of habitat.

Fossil remains show two possible ways in which birds might have begun flying. One theory suggests that when birds' two-footed reptile predecessors ran on their long hind legs, they flapped their shorter fore-limbs and used their tails to aid the speed and balance of their progress. At some period they became warm-blooded and gradually their scales, chemically similar to feathers, lengthened and frayed and were able to grow into light, lift-assisting plumage. An ability to glide, acquired in this way, gradually improved into soaring, powered flight, made possible by flapping the increasingly efficient wings and by the reduction of the heavy bones in the tail. But the most widely held belief, supported by the remains of *Archaeopteryx*, is that the flight of birds developed when their reptilian ancestors took to the trees. So that they could move easily from tree to tree there grew a greater difference between the structure and use of their front and rear limbs, the forearms keeping fingers which had hooks for grasping. Jumping from branch to branch developed the wings, at first for gliding then for powered flight. Other reptiles, the Pterosaurs, became able to fly by developing a double fold of skin on the side of the body between the limbs, but they were less efficient and have long since become extinct. Bats were more successful with a similar development of patagial (wing) membrane used for flying, but they are mammals and developed along a different evolutionary branch of the ancestral tree of the animal kingdom.

Most of the species of ancient birds no longer exist as recognizable forms. Many had become over-specialized and failed to adapt to the ever-changing climate and environment or had been wiped out by more efficient kinds of birds or by predators. There is, unfortunately, a gap of thirty million years between our first known bird and those whose fossils have been found in the rocks of the Cretaceous period. This was a time when birds were becoming well established, and by the time Man came on the world scene there was a richer variety of birds than there is now. But birds still seem to be the most successful of the vertebrate animals (that is, those which have a backbone) with some 25,000 species and subspecies, compared with a similarly combined total of 15,000 kinds of mammals and about the same number of kinds of fishes, though these latter are the more abundant.

Of the world total of birds, more than three hundred species are threatened with extinction long before they might be due to disappear in the course of evolution. In the last two hundred years the disappearance of species which cannot be replaced has been greatly speeded up by the activities of Man as he has become very much more destructive and increasingly numerous in parts of the world that were once thinly populated. Those most easily harmed by Man were, of course, the first to go and others are evidently in danger of the same fate. Many Orders of birds lost their need to fly because there were few or no enemies from which to escape, and some of these still survive. Some, like the Ostrich, forsook flying for being able to run extremely quickly; some, like the penguins, turned their wings into flippers which enabled them to 'fly' under water in pursuit of their food; some, like the Kiwis, lived in forests on isolated islands where there were no land carnivores from which they needed to escape by flight – until the advent of Man and his animals.

No fewer than 127 species and distinct races have become extinct since the time of the Dodo, the first bird ever to be recorded as being lost to the world, because of Man, some three hundred years ago. When something is said to be 'as dead as the Dodo' it really does mean that nobody will ever see its like again. This turkey-sized bird, with the appearance of a huge, wingless pigeon, lived on the lonely island of Mauritius, where it had lost its need to fly. Then exploring European seamen found an easy source of food in the big, clumsy creature until they killed the last of the Dodos in 1681. The several kinds of Moa of New Zealand – some of them stood as high as 10 ft (3.1 m) – met a similar fate at the hands of the first human settlers of that country,

A stuffed specimen of the Great Auk in a museum in Iceland where the last pair of these large, flightless sea birds was killed by hungry sailors in 1844.

the Polynesians who came from islands to the north about a thousand years ago. The birds were numerous and men were at first few, so that moa-hunting was still an important part of Maori life until a few centuries ago when all of these big, defenceless birds were destroyed.

Another large, helpless bird that could not escape from Man was the Great Auk of the sub-arctic regions of the North Atlantic. The last pair of the flightless sea birds was killed on Eldey Island, Iceland, on 4 June 1844. In still more modern times the most dramatic case of the extinction of a bird species was that of the Passenger Pigeon of North America. Flocks several miles long, one estimated by reliable ornithologists as containing no fewer than a thousand million birds, could still be seen in the nineteenth century, but the relentlessly increasing activity of humans had caused the complete destruction of all the wild birds by the early part of this century, the last known specimen dying in Cincinnati Zoo in 1914. Man has been called the most dangerous animal on earth. He has been particularly destructive to birds.

3 The Classification and Naming of Birds

*I*n the world there are about 8,600 different species of birds. As with all other living things, they are so varied and have so many different local names that an international system is needed for classifying and naming them. Such a system, using Latin, was introduced in 1758 by the Swedish naturalist Carl von Linné whose name is more familiar Latinized as Carolus Linnaeus.

The scientific arrangement of birds first places them into Orders, such as the Order Passeriformes (perching birds). An Order includes all the Families which are considered to be closely related. A Family, such as the Paridae (tits), comprises smaller groups, called Genera, which together appear to be distinctive. Between some Orders and Families and some Families and Genera, birds can be grouped into Suborders and Subfamilies because they have some similar characteristics.

The natural unit of classification is the Species because this is the lowest division of groups of birds that will not normally interbreed with other kinds. In many bird books and ornithological publications, a Species is referred to by two Latin names, usually given after the common name, when they are printed in italics. The first Latin name, with a capital initial, denotes the Genus and the second name, used without a capital initial, identifies the exact Species, despite its having different common names in different countries e.g. Coal Tit *Parus ater* in Britain, Zwarte Mees *Parus ater* in the Netherlands and Московка *Parus ater* in Russia. Subspecies, which are geographical races that have developed some difference in plumage or size or both, are identified by a third Latin name. Where their ranges overlap, Subspecies may interbreed.

The name which sometimes is given after the Latin name, especially in scientific books, is that of the zoologist who first described the type. Many birds have been collected by zoologists in order to show a type specimen or to be used for study collections. These specimens are called 'skins' and the extensive collection of the British Museum (Natural History) is housed at Tring, Hertfordshire.

PREVIOUS PAGES Great Tits making good use of peanuts in a container hung just outside a kitchen window.

An example of classification

ORDER: *Passeriformes* Perching birds, with toes adapted for grasping a branch. There are 27 Orders of birds in the world (18 in the UK). Passeriformes comprise about 5,110 of the world total of about 8,600 species.

SUBORDER: *Oscines* Singing birds, with a particular muscular arrangement of the larynx. One of four suborders and the only one represented in our region of the world.

FAMILY: *Paridae* One of the 58 world families of birds (20 families in the UK).

SUBFAMILY: *Parinae* The typical tits (titmice), which nest in holes and are found in Europe, North Africa, Asia and North America.

GENUS: *Parus* Comprising of 46 species of true tits breeding in the world.

SPECIES: *Parus ater* The Coal Tit, one of six species of true tits breeding in the British Isles.

SUB-SPECIES: *P. a. britannicus* Sharpe & Dresser, 1871. The British Coal Tit. Breeds in Britain and north-east Ireland. White patches on cheek and nape are less bright than those on the Continental race *P. a. ater*.

P. a. hibernicus Ogilvie-Grant The Irish Coal Tit. Breeds in Ireland. Generally has a yellowish tint in the white areas of the cheek and nape.

Sixteen other races of the Coal Tit, distributed across Europe, North Africa and Asia as far as Japan, have been described and named.

The Topography of a Bird
showing the main features of a Whinchat

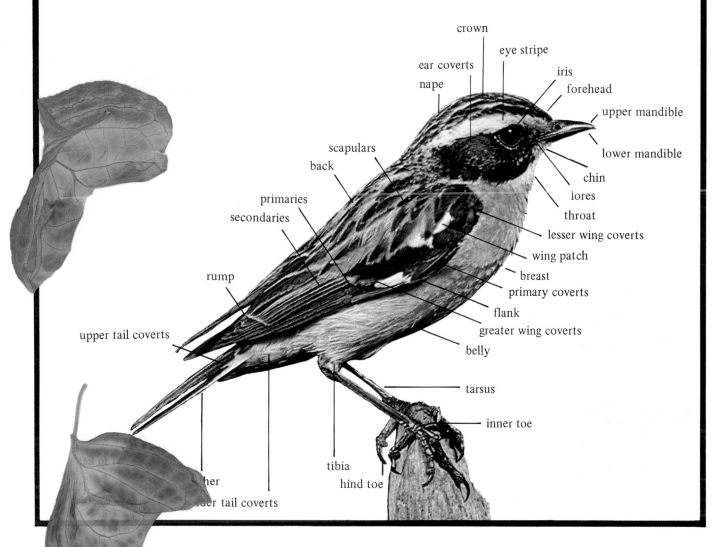

crown

eye stripe

ear coverts

iris

nape

forehead

upper mandible

lower mandible

scapulars

chin

back

lores

primaries

throat

secondaries

lesser wing coverts

wing patch

breast

rump

primary coverts

flank

greater wing coverts

upper tail coverts

belly

tarsus

inner toe

tibia

...her

hind toe

...der tail coverts

...ssification of all birds cannot be rigid and mu... ...on a large amount of guesswork for want of sufficient evidence from the past, and must also cause argument, ornithologists in the field and in museums do at least know what birds they are talking and writing about. By comparison, there is much less discipline in the use of everyday names and there are many species which continue to be commonly referred to by quite different names in different parts of the country: Stone Curlew=Thickknee=Norfolk Plover; Lapwing=Peewit=Green Plover – these are examples of the many multi-named species.

The naming of birds is especially confused in the Englishspeaking world. Early settlers from Britain, seeing many birds completely new to them, called some of them by comfortable, homely names if in any way they resembled birds of the old country. In Britain, the name 'Robin' immediately brings to mind our best-loved, best-known, little garden bird. But 'Robin' to the North American means a bird as big as our Blackbird, dark brown above and bright rusty red below. In New Zealand, settlers clearing their way into the strange, new forest saw small birds poking about on the dark woodland floor having all the friendly characteristics, shape, posture and big eyes of the Robin they had left behind. They dubbed the new bird 'Robin' even though it was noticeably bigger and was almost all black with no red at all in its plumage. There are Robins, too, in Australia, extraordinarily colourful birds of many species. They are smaller than our bird and, since they are all, in fact, Flycatchers, which do not need to be good walkers, they all have short legs. They do, however, have something of the shape of the European Robin and several species have coloured breasts. Australians can talk about their Scarlet Robins and Rose, Pink, Flame, Yellow and many other kinds of Robins with colourful first names.

As birdwatchers travel more to each other's countries there is a growing dissatisfaction with the way we have given common names to birds. As in any volatile language, accepted bird names are those in common use and they have been given for a variety of practical, convenient or semi-scientific reasons. Birds have been named from the way they sing, fly, build nests, arrive and depart with the seasons, from distinctive parts of their body or limbs, from their colours, habitat, native country or just out of nostalgia or to honour a friend. But as different genera, species and subspecies were discovered, mostly beyond the Old World, the need for names which would describe birds more exactly gave rise to highly unwieldy ones. There is, for instance, a tiny bird with the long name of Red-fronted Flower-pecker Weaver Finch. Perhaps fortunately for the birdwatchers of West Central Africa, where it lives in dense forests, it is rare. Its scientific name is the mere *Parmoptila rubifrons*. Such long vernacular names, necessary as they may be, are by no means unusual: but before you could say 'There goes a Thick-billed Red-tailed Greenbul,' the bird may well have flown out of sight. Short cuts and abbreviations are, of course, used for birds often seen and discussed. Down-to-earth Australian birdwatchers, when talking about their very common Black-faced Cuckoo-shrike, use a combination of initials and say 'bifcus'.

In Europe, where birdwatching has been popular for the longest time, we some time ago identified all our native birds and gave them common names. We have not needed to add to the names to differentiate our birds from similar species in other countries and this has resulted in unfairness to our friends overseas. We still talk about 'the Cuckoo' but there is a total of 125 species of Cuckoos in the world and

The Great Spotted Woodpecker is one of the most colourful species. If food is provided regularly, it can be attracted to our gardens. As well as peanuts, it will come to any kind of fat, which can be spread on a post.

sixty-four of them include that word in their common name. We have 'the Cormorant' and 'the Shag', while in other countries the thirty species in this family of Phalacrocoracidae have to have longer names. Our Cormorant, *Phalacrocorax carbo*, has a wide distribution round the world and is called the Great Cormorant in North America and parts of South-east Asia, the Black Shag in New Zealand, the Black Cormorant in Australia, the White-necked Cormorant in East Africa and the Large Cormorant in India and Thailand. Reorganization in the use of common names for widespread species is having to occur, however. For example, instead of Bonaparte's Sandpiper we now use the American name of White-rumped Sandpiper; instead of Red-backed Sandpiper the Americans now use our name of Dunlin.

4 British Breeding Birds in their Habitats

For their survival birds depend most of all on the availability of the right kinds of food. The abundance and variety of food depend on climate and what we do to the earth's surface and its vegetation. In Britain, birds are fortunate; their many different diets can be met because of the variety of weather and habitats. As offshore islands of the continent of Europe, where summer and winter differences of temperature and rainfall are more likely to be extreme, Britain and Ireland are warmed throughout the year by the Gulf Stream, and the mainly Atlantic origin of our weather gives us a mostly moist climate – the annual average rainfall ranges from 200 in. (5,080 mm) at one part of the Lake District to the 20 in. (508 mm) of coastal Suffolk. Four-fifths of our country is farmed and most of our crops, vegetable and animal, are very varied.

Throughout the year, therefore, the native population of our birds is at least as rich in variety and number as it is in any other comparably small area elsewhere in north-west Europe but, being in a temperate zone – that is, with mainly westerly winds bringing changeable weather and having low temperatures in winter – we cannot have as many as the tropics. The 470 species, of which about two hundred breed regularly, that have been recorded in Britain and Ireland compare with 1,700 species in Colombia, the world's most bird-rich country. Our present population is the result, as in other countries, of millions of years of geological changes and changes in climate which are still continuing – we are losing some species and gaining new ones. But most dramatically influencing the number and kind of birds we have now has been the effect, over the past few hundred years, of Man upon the surface of our country. Only some of our mountain-tops and sea cliffs remain unaltered by our action.

We have greatly reduced the numbers of several of our insect-eating species and we are continuing to do so. The present situation is not wholly harmful to birds, however, and the number of species breeding in Britain is in fact increasing at the present time. Only one, the Kentish Plover, a species which can live in many other parts of the world in any case, has ceased to nest on our coasts since 1940, while ten new ones have become established in that time. The breeding range of a few species, still numerous elsewhere, no longer extends to Britain but through no fault of our own. In this country, our understanding of the value of wetlands has allowed the return of six species of marshland breeding birds which, through drainage of their habitat and callous shooting, we had wiped out in the 1800s.

Some kinds of birds have become more numerous than perhaps we would like. These are the more adaptable, highly successful species that have been quick to learn to live off Man's waste and agricultural activities and include

PREVIOUS PAGES A group of colourful Shelducks – common throughout Britain perhaps because man finds them almost inedible. The birds' young are formed into crêches cared for by one or two adults while most of the parents fly away to moult.

gulls, crows, Starlings, finches and House Sparrows. Others, like the tits, Robins and other members of the thrush family, are maintaining their good numbers with the help of our growing affection for familiar garden birds. We get pleasure from feeding and watching them and, with the much-increased heat now generated by every town and village, more resident birds are able to survive harsh winters than previously.

About sixty of our two hundred breeding species are summer visitors which spend the rest of the year in, or travelling to and from, winter quarters, mostly in Africa. These are the kinds of birds whose survival has depended on being able to enjoy the best of both worlds: their annual return journeys are inherited behaviour which developed long ago in conditions of geography and climate very different from those of today. For many species, their migration continues to be necessary because their particular kinds of food are not available to them in winter in the northerly areas where they spend the breeding season.

Britain's geographical position enables its millions of migrant warblers, flycatchers, swallows and other small birds which depend on insects to get to Spain and Africa for the winter with relative ease. Populations of hardier species

House Martins can often be seen flying to and from eaves of buildings where they regularly make their nests as this one has.

31

whose summer homes are farther north and east, depend on our milder climate in the non-breeding season. Not for long, here, do ice and snow hide away the worms and insects and other invertebrates to be found in our gardens, farms, marshes and estuaries, while a good supply of seeds and fruits is generally available. The number of thrushes, Starlings and finches that come across the North Sea each autumn is vast. They join the foraging flocks of their British cousins which do not need to migrate and which spend all their lives with us. At most times of the year, too, but especially in the periods of March to May and July to November, passage migrants use Britain as a stopover, many staying for a few hours or a few weeks while they feed to replace fuel used up already on their journey between summer and winter quarters.

Several British ornithologists, notably the late James Fisher, E.M. Nicholson, John Parslow and Dr J.T.R. Sharrock, with others working for the British Trust for Ornithology and the British Ornithologists' Union, have assessed the breeding populations of the land birds of Great Britain and Ireland. It appears that, in very round figures, these 120,750 square miles (312,740 square km) support a total population of some 120 millions. This is an average of just over two birds per acre (0.4 per hectare), though by far the most are to be found in gardens and parks, for birds are scarce on high mountains and moors. The variety of birds able to nest in our many different habitats is also high at just over two hundred. Any new species attempting to breed here, extending its range and becoming more adaptable to fit in with the slowly changing climate, benefits from our mainly protective attitude, though this is toned down by our mechanical attack on the earth and our chemical attack on the plant and insect populations. Many species are able to survive in Britain and Ireland because of the existence of reserves managed by national bodies like the Royal Society for the Protection of Birds whose membership has increased enormously in the past twenty-five years, the Society for the Promotion of Nature Conservation, the Nature Conservancy Council, the many county Naturalists' Trusts and the Irish Wildbird Conservancy. On one of the smaller reserves, Minsmere in Suffolk, owned by the RSPB, one hundred different species can breed within its 1,500 acres (600 hectares). This is a greater variety than can be found within a similarly small area elsewhere in western Europe and includes some rare species only able to breed because the special living conditions which they need are provided for them.

About three-quarters of Britain's bird population are the common ones we expect to see in our fields and farmland, hedgerows and gardens. These are members of the families of thrushes, crows and finches and birds like Dunnocks and

Well known as one of Britain's most common birds, the Starling has been spread by Europeans to countries throughout the world. In some places it has become a nuisance and competes with local species. This picture shows a female, which is distinguished from the male by the pinkish base to her yellow bill. The Starling's metallic colours and light spots show it to be a more beautiful bird than it is given credit for.

BELOW A resplendent male Pheasant. Rough corners are left on large estates so that they can feed and the females nest there. Such coverts also provide food and nesting sites for many small birds.

Skylarks, as well as the two most common birds that Man has spread around the world, Starlings and House Sparrows. Because of Britain's strict laws for bird protection, our more humane attitude to wildlife and our improved standard of living, we no longer accept that little birds may be killed for food or sport. It is a long time since four-and-twenty Blackbirds were baked in a pie and the British Trust for Ornithology considers that we may now have more than seven million pairs of these delightful songsters distributed throughout Britain and Ireland. As their fear of Man grows less, cultivation of farmland increases and there are more food-rich gardens, these once-shy birds of the woodlands have within the last hundred years become one of our most abundant land birds.

It is probably also a long time since British housewives took the trouble to cook still smaller birds like House Sparrows, a species not protected by law, for a meal, but this is not the case in many Continental countries where finches, larks and other small species are lawful game birds and their shattered corpses are proudly hung around the belts of sportsmen. Throughout the year, the average number and variety of birds seen in an ordinary lane in Britain will be quite high. We are, however, keen killers of wildfowl and, as is the case in many other countries, the number of shot-gun owners is increasing. As a result, however, so is the membership of the Wildfowlers' Association of Great Britain and Ireland, which is able to exercise a greater control over shooting. Despite the fact that, unlike North America, Australia, New Zealand and some other countries, we do not place a legal limit on the numbers which may be shot, our populations of ducks are not growing smaller. Indeed, because of improving conservation in the breeding season and the use of new gravel-pits and reservoirs, many species are, in fact, increasing.

The shooting of land game birds like Pheasants and Partridges, however, continues to have a very marked effect upon the numbers of our birds of prey, and local populations of hawks and owls lessen according to the numbers of keepers who kill them illegally in the mistaken belief that they are protecting their game birds. Fewer hooked-beaked birds of prey are to be found in the south-eastern quarter of England, where there are more intensively managed game preserves than in other parts of the country. But in these parts other species, especially song birds, fare well because of the larger amount of hedges, copses and rough corners left as coverts for the Pheasants and Partridges. And doves and finches are helped, especially in the winter, by being able to feed on the seed and pellets distributed at regular sites on their preserves by the keepers, many of whom take pleasure from this fact.

Birds of Marshes, Lakes and Rivers

Among the wide variety of habitats to be found in the British Isles, wetlands support the richest communities of plants and animals. But environments of this type have long been spoiled by human activity, and the bird populations of our marshes and lakes are less varied and abundant than they were in medieval times.

In this country the growth and decline of forests, the advance and retreat of glaciers and the fall and rise of the surface of the earth had left large areas of peaty marshlands, moorland bogs and lochs and blocked-off estuaries. Storks bred in Scotland in the fifteenth century, Spoonbills were breeding in Sussex (and at Fulham!) in the next century, still later in Wales, and in East Anglia until the mid-1600s. In the fens, the relatively few marshmen supported their families on the wildlife around them, being particularly skilful at catching waders in nets, but this probably had very little effect upon the bird populations.

But then came the Industrial Revolution and the growing human population demanded the use of more and more land. Marshes were drained and the numbers of highly specialized birds that could not adapt to other habitats were much reduced. Also disastrous was that the birds became in increasing demand for food. Plovers, Ruffs and many other kinds of waders, by the scores of dozens, were trapped and sent to market, and to banquets held in mansions on the growing number of country estates. Then, as certain species became rare, the birds were more eagerly sought after by sportsmen or collectors for museums or were shot simply out of curiosity. By the end of the 1800s, six reed-bed species had ceased to breed.

Because of our closeness to mainland Europe, none of these wetland species is obliged to live only in Britain and, given the opportunity, they could re-establish themselves in these islands from stock still in good number on the Continent. Since the early part of the present century this has in some cases come about. Landowners now have a better appreciation of their responsibilities, there is a general improvement in the public attitude towards wildlife, and large new reed-beds were created as a result of war-time defensive flooding – this has helped all of the birds

OPPOSITE A Grey Heron and young at a typical tree-top nest. It is a good site, near water, where they can catch food such as eels, of which they eat a lot, other fish and frogs.

we lost in the last century to make a come-back. In our small country, where we are now very conscious of the urgent need for nature reserves, almost every reed-bed of good size is protected for the benefit of its wildlife.

One of the most important species that breeds again in Britain is the Marsh Harrier. It is one of our rarest birds of prey: only Shetland's Snowy Owls and the recently scarce Montagu's Harrier are fewer. This large hawk – the females, bigger than the males, have a wing span of about 4 ft 4 in. (1300 mm) – was a common sight in our wetlands until the early 1800s but had ceased to breed in England and Wales by the end of the century and in Ireland after 1917. A pair attempted to nest again in Norfolk in 1908 and occasionally thereafter, but breeding did not become regular until 1927. The best years in their present period of recovery were 1957 and 1958 when about twelve pairs nested in East Anglia and another five to six did so elsewhere. Then, for reasons which are not entirely clear, numbers of breeding pairs declined dramatically in the 1960s to about six pairs, falling still further to one to four pairs in the early 1970s. A slow improvement is again occurring, with eight pairs, almost all in Suffolk coastal marshes, nesting with high success in 1976.

As many as 135 healthy young Marsh Harriers have been fledged from the RSPB's reserve at Minsmere since they began to nest there in 1955. Allowing a high death-rate among juveniles this productivity alone should have resulted by now in a reasonably large breeding population in Britain. One of the important reasons for this not being so may be that many are shot. Young birds and some adults are migratory and while we may protect them here we cannot do so in, or on their way to, winter quarters in north-west Africa. A nestling ringed in Norfolk was killed in Morocco two years later. A juvenile which had been found starving in a Coypu trap on a neighbouring marsh was restored to health by RSPB wardens and ringed when it was released, in late September; this bird was killed on the River Senegal in Mauritania in the following April.

The adult female Marsh Harrier is mainly brown with a creamy head and patches on the forewing. She looks like a common Buzzard but, in common with all the harrier species, has a longer tail and holds up her wings in a shallow V when gliding. The noticeably smaller male has a grey tail and wing patches and is a spectacular performer of aerial acrobatics. In his courtship flight he dives from a great height, twisting and turning then zooms up to loop the loop or do a barrel roll. He frequently has two mates and is a keen parent, passing food to a mate in a skilful mid-air manoeuvre when, in response to his calling, she rises from the nest deep in the reed-bed. The prey includes many small Rabbits taken by surprise by the low-flying male in his wide

A female Marsh Harrier with her downy young at a nest hidden deep in a reed-bed. One of Britain's rarest birds, it was lost as a breeding bird during the last century through being shot and through the destruction of its special habitat. A few pairs returned early in this century when protection began to be given to them. Now less than a dozen pairs nest in heavily guarded sites.

hunting territory. On the marsh, the harriers take other small rodents, especially water voles, which are common, and the young of waders, ducks and other water birds. They exercise little effective control over eastern England's population of Coypus, the big vegetarian rodents brought to this country from South America before the war to be bred for their fur, nutria. The Coypu breeds rapidly and produces many young, and when some escaped from fur farms near Norwich a huge wild population built up in East Anglia's reed-beds and fens. A trapping campaign and a long period of icy conditions brought about the destruction of some 100,000 of these animals in the winter of 1962–3 but their numbers soon reached their previous level again. On a wetland bird reserve, the Coypus are trapped to prevent the destruction of large areas of vegetation, the loss of water through holes the animals make in banks, and because they like to climb on to birds' nests to preen their fur. Like all foreign creatures introduced to a strange land where there is no place for them in the local ecology, if they do not fail entirely they flourish only at the expense of the local plants and animals.

Another large raptor (bird of prey) now nesting regularly after ill-treatment by Man had prevented it from doing so since the beginning of this century is the Osprey. Breeding began again on Scotland's Speyside in 1955 (perhaps in 1954) by one pair, and protection has helped the population to increase to some fifteen pairs at the present time. These fish hawks, which also occasionally take common water birds like Moorhens, are still under the threat of egg-collectors and their eyries (nests), all in Scotland, have to be guarded night and day.

Large raptors of the wetlands, at the top of the prey-predator pyramid, have few natural enemies in their breeding habitats. One which has been shown possibly to be significant is the Bittern. Itself another of those species which we had wiped out and which has now been given the chance to begin living again in our reed marshes, it has been known to attack Marsh Harriers' nests and to destroy their young. Bitterns are omnivorous (that is, they will eat all types of food), the young leave the nest when about half-grown and, like their parents, eat anything of manageable size that they come across. In a 400-acre (160-hectare) reed-bed, where, apparently, the fourteen pairs of Bitterns are the optimum number, battles between Harriers and Bitterns have frequently been observed. An adult Harrier can only defend its nest by swooping from above at the enemy attempting to rob it; it dare not make contact with the Bittern's powerful beak, raised like an upthrust short-sword.

Now that Man is no longer the Bittern's worst enemy, the rate of increase of this species will depend largely upon

The Osprey, a large, fish-eating hawk was a species so much persecuted that for many years in the first part of this century no Ospreys bred in Britain. Now more than a dozen pairs breed in the Scottish Highlands.

whether long periods of severe frost occur. The British Bittern population, which is found in scattered sites from Lancashire to Kent, highest numbers being in Suffolk, is sedentary, and when their food is locked away under ice and snow many die. But the recent series of mild winters has been good for these birds, and their un-birdlike, booming spring song sometimes begins as early as late January. Bitterns are more often heard than seen, at least up to mid-June when their courtship and territorial calling ceases but, where several birds occupy a marsh, a group of two to six may be watched making clumsy, grunting, nuptial flights in April and May. The best chance of seeing them is from one of the permanent wooden hides on a marshland bird reserve like Minsmere or Leighton Moss when one, golden and dark brown like a bunch of winter reeds, emerges stealthily from cover to pick up an item of prey or walks warily across a clearing.

A much more easily observed and larger relative of the Bittern is the Grey Heron. While it, too, feeds on anything it can manage, it stands, motionless, out in the open in shallow ponds or at the edges of ditches. This species is also seriously affected by periods of severe frost and after the bitter winter of 1940 it was estimated that a quarter of the British population, then four thousand pairs, had perished. A rapid recovery was followed by another set-back during the arctic winter of 1962–3, but numbers are high again and the present population is distributed all over Britain and Ireland, with fewest in north and east Scotland and north-east England. Heronries, of two to sometimes a hundred nests, are normally sited in tall trees, the species being less important than that the wood or copse should be within a short flight of good feeding sites, for which estuaries are particularly favoured. The success and continuance of a colony is much affected by disturbance from people, especially gamekeepers and others with interests in fish stocks, and by tree-felling operations. Heronries have sometimes been forced to move to another site by the growing success of a neighbouring colony of Rooks. Where trees are scarce but the fishing is good, as in Scotland, herons may nest on the side of a cliff or on the ground on an islet in a loch. They have nested on the stones on the treeless wastes of Dungeness in Kent, and there is a reed-bed colony in Hertfordshire and one in Suffolk.

Like the Bittern, the Grey Heron is well equipped to deal with the messy effects of killing and swallowing a favourite prey, the Eel, which may cover the bird's head and neck feathers with slime. After rubbing the affected parts on the patches of powder down, of which it has three pairs on its flanks and underparts (Bitterns have two pairs) the feathers are rearranged with the special comb-like claw of the middle toe of each foot. When the remains of the powder

This female Bittern is being forced to disgorge food by her chick which tugs at her beak. With protection and the restoration of reed-beds in Britain, these birds are becoming more numerous after being eliminated in the last century.

have dried and have been shaken out, the toilet is completed by re-oiling each feather with the bill. The oil for this is obtained from the gland under the tail coverts.

Rarer fish-eating birds of British waters are the Black-throated and Red-throated Divers which breed in lochs in north-west Scotland. A few pairs of the latter species also nest in Northern Ireland. They are more likely to be seen around our coasts in winter, many of them no doubt from other European breeding areas. These are our most primitive forms of birds, with legs set at the rear of their bodies to make them excellent divers from the surface of the water and fast swimmers below, but poor walkers on land so that their nests are usually placed close to the shore of the loch.

Our Grebes are built in a similar way, for the same purpose of catching fish. Largest in size, most common and widespread, except in the extreme west, and steadily increasing in numbers, the Great Crested Grebe is becoming less shy of people. The remarkable courtship dance can generally be seen quite easily in spring when a pair of birds standing face to face, almost on tiptoe on the water, wag their chestnut-fringed, black-crested heads at each other. The smallest member of the Grebe family, the

A Black-throated Diver. This species nests near the water because despite its being a superb swimmer and fish catcher it is ungainly on land.

39

Little Grebe, is even more widely spread throughout Britain but is not increasing. It, too, has a reddish patch on the side of the upper neck in spring, making it quite distinctive, but it prefers rush- and reed-growing lakes and quite small waters and is generally less easily seen than the larger species. Its presence can often be detected by its remarkable trilling cry, known as 'whinnying'. The Black-necked Grebe is our scarcest bird of this group: there are only some twenty pairs breeding, mostly on their own, in a few sites between north Scotland and south Kent. The Slavonian Grebe is less rare, but its breeding range is not as wide, for it is practically limited to inland lochs in Scotland where there are some sixty pairs. Their summer plumage is oily red on the neck and body. In winter, when they are grey and white, they are difficult to distinguish from the Black-necked Grebe but their rather longer necks make them appear a little less dumpy.

In these days when wild places are becoming fewer and more likely to be disturbed by Man, it is encouraging for birdwatchers as well as wildfowlers to know that several of Britain's duck species are increasing their numbers while others are keeping up good populations. Mallard are abundant everywhere; Teal, our smallest duck, breed in most counties while the once-scarce Gadwall, introduced into different areas by sportsmen, is doing very well, in some

A Great Crested Grebe on its nest. Its newly hatched chick has climbed on to its back, a position the chick will often adopt when its parent is swimming.

fenland areas even outnumbering Mallard. The heavy-billed but colourful Shoveler, whose western European and British population greatly increased in the first half of the present century, is to be found in most low-lying marshes. The Pintail, gracefully slender-necked, is much less numerous and nests in scattered sites in Scotland and southern England, and here and there in Ireland.

Fast-flying ducks are generally not easy to identify in flight. The Wigeon helps with its large area of white on the forewing and distinctive 'wheeoo' call. It breeds mainly on high wetland in Scotland, also in north-west Yorkshire and occasionally elsewhere in England and Wales. Outside the breeding season, populations of all these 'dabbling' ducks, which feed from the surface and whose females all wear unobtrusive brown plumage, rise and fall widely with local migrations and the arrival of wintering flocks from the Continent. Our one regularly breeding surface feeder which is wholly migratory is the Garganey, a slightly larger relative of the Teal and recognized in flight by its pale blue forewing; the male has a conspicuous curve of white over the eye. British Garganeys winter in tropical Africa and are early-returning migrants, sometimes arriving at the end of February or the beginning of March when they may well be the first spring birds a birdwatcher records.

Compared with these species, the female Shelduck is brightly coloured like her mate. Nesting in holes, most often in Rabbit burrows or, if none is available, under a building, fallen tree or thick bush (rarely in a hole in a standing tree), she does not need earth-brown, camouflage plumage. The Shelduck is large, mainly white with black on the wings and belly, a bright chestnut band across the breast and a dark green head. It is to be found around all of the coasts of the British Isles and is very common, perhaps because Man finds it almost inedible. The nest may be a mile or more from water and the large brood of ducklings, looking like old-fashioned, striped humbugs, are led by one or both parents on the long walk to the comparative safety of an estuary or mere. As with most families of ducklings, the death-rate is heavy but, unlike other species, broods unite to form a 'crèche', sometimes numbering up to fifty, which are in the care of only one or two parents, or more if the crèche is extra large. Another feature of Shelduck behaviour is that in July and August most of our birds fly to the broad sands in the coastal corner of western Denmark and Germany where huge numbers gather to moult. Smaller numbers use Bridgwater Bay in Somerset as a safe area for this vital period in the birds' annual cycle.

Of the ducks which dive from the surface to feed on a variety of small animal life and vegetable matter, by far the most common and widespread in Britain and Ireland is the Tufted Duck. It is present throughout the year and has

An elegant, well-named Pintail. This one is a drake. His mate, as with other surface-feeding ducks, is a much duller brown and camouflaged to protect her nest, where she incubates her eggs.

The drake Tufted Duck. These birds are becoming numerous and widespread throughout Britain, readily making use of gravel-pits and other water-filled excavations by roadsides.

41

taken great advantage of the many new reservoirs and gravel-pits; a few pairs may be seen alongside even the newest motorways in flooded 'borrow pits' where plant and animal life has begun to establish itself. Much less widespread, in smaller but increasing numbers, is the Pochard, whose diet is more vegetarian than the related Tufted Duck. It is a smart, red-headed bird, breeding mostly around well-established waters which are fringed with reeds and other aquatic plants. The Scaup, looking like a larger Tufted Duck but with the males having a grey instead of a black back, is a bird of the fresh waters of arctic and sub-arctic tundra, though one or more pairs nest in a scattered way in Scotland. Another rare breeding duck, the Wood Duck, was introduced from North America; the Mandarin, brought here from China, has established a larger wild population, mainly in southern England, with smaller numbers in Scotland. These are birds of woodland ponds but may occur on marshes.

Our two 'saw-bills', diving ducks so called because of the saw-like 'teeth' along the edges of their bills which enable them to grip fish, are the Red-breasted Merganser and the Goosander. Both nest in good numbers by lakes and rivers in Scotland and have increased their range into northern England, the former also into north Wales. Their plumages are rather similar, especially in winter, when the Merganser is much more likely to be seen at sea. The Goosander is a noticeably bigger bird and in summer the male lacks the chestnut breast and conspicuous, untidy crest of the other member of the genus.

The wholly black ducks which may be seen in groups, forming large 'rafts' moving up and down with the waves off our coasts during the year, are Common Scoters. They dive for molluscs, but where they breed, in small numbers by freshwater lochs in north Scotland and the northern isles and, in greater numbers, by Irish loughs, they also eat worms, insects and some vegetation. Flocks sometimes include birds with white wing patches. These are Velvet Scoters which breed in the more northerly parts of north-west Europe; a pair was thought to have bred in Shetland in 1945. A much more numerous sea duck, which is only rarely seen in rivers and lakes, is the Eider, famous for its down for which it is 'farmed' in Iceland and with which it lines its nest. It feeds like the scoters but may be recognized as a much larger duck, generally in smaller groups, distinctly Grecian-nosed in profile, the adult male appearing mainly white above and black below, with a black head and tail. Eiders breed in good and increasing numbers, in colonies around the coasts of Scotland and the isles, also in north-east and north-west England and Northern Ireland. Outside the breeding season they are seen with increasing frequency around all our coasts. They are less shy than our

ABOVE These Canada Geese have a large family. They are becoming increasingly common and form large grazing flocks in the winter. They are particularly numerous in East Anglian meadows and meres.

Whooper Swans, one of Britain's largest birds, can be distinguished from the common Mute Swan by their straighter neck and the yellow on their bill. A few pairs nest in northern Scotland but most of our birds are winter visitors from breeding grounds in Iceland, northern Scandinavia, and arctic Russia.

other sea ducks and may feed very close to the shore.

Two species of geese breed in Britain, one of which, the Greylag, is native. By the beginning of the First World War shooting had brought the population to a dangerously low level but now fairly good numbers from the original stock hold their own in northern Scotland and the western isles. There, and elsewhere in Britain, numbers have been considerably increased by wild populations of birds introduced by the Wildfowlers' Association.

The Canada Goose, which was introduced and semi-domesticated at least three hundred years ago when it was kept in London's St James's Park, has spread of its own accord, as well as with the help of landowners and wildfowlers, to most waters of England and Wales, the southern half of Scotland and north-east Ireland. It is a large goose and in Britain has no need to make the migratory flights which are a sight to behold in spring and autumn in its native North America. In East Anglia, where it has become abundant and feeds a good deal in grazing meadows in competition with sheep and cattle, as well as on barley stubbles, very large numbers gather at favourite sites. The most noteworthy flock is at Holkham, in Norfolk, where up to two thousand live in association with other introduced wildfowl. Among these are Egyptian Geese which now breed wild elsewhere in that county and in neighbouring Suffolk. Being large, they look like geese but are in fact ducks of the sub-family *Anatinae* and have the large, white wing patches of their related Shelducks.

Swans are the largest birds to be seen on our wetlands and rivers. The Mute and Whooper swans are of about the same size but the latter is a rare, occasional breeder in Britain, nesting only in north Scotland. It may be recognized by its generally straighter neck and yellow patch on the bill and is seen here mainly as a winter visitor. The much smaller Bewick's Swan, also with some yellow on the bill, is entirely a winter visitor, its breeding range being in the arctic tundra of Siberia in the USSR.

Mute Swans nest by almost any waters with suitable rich, shallow margins and are common throughout the British Isles except in the extreme north-west of Scotland and some of the islands. They increased considerably in the present century and, with annual increases and decreases due to the availability of food in winters, their breeding population is now fairly stable at about four thousand pairs out of a total, including immature and other non-breeding birds, of nearly twenty thousand. Except that owners of grazing land and others with an interest in waterside meadows and lawns may dislike them for the amount of grass they eat and foul, the build-up of our wild and semi-wild population has been helped by our increasing affection for them. Once an important food, especially in medieval times when they were kept for this purpose under strict regulations laid down by the Crown, these swans are now rarely eaten and are admired for the beauty and grace they add to a city park or country scene.

The affectionate legend that all Mute Swans belong to the reigning monarch arises from a practice which was already well established by the twelfth century. At that time all swans which roamed free and were not kept, by royal grant, pinioned (that is, with their wings clipped to stop them flying away) on private estates were claimed and taken by the Royal Swan-master. Swan-owners were required by law to pursue and capture any birds which escaped from their care and each had to mark his birds with his own arrangement of nicks on the beak. The name of an inn, The Swan with Two Necks, was a misunderstanding of this old practice which, by the time of Queen Elizabeth I had so extended that more than nine hundred different swan marks were receiving royal recognition. In 1590, the Queen seized 440 unmarked birds out of a total of five hundred in the Abbotsbury Swannery in Dorset. This famous herd, which was in existence at least as early as the fourteenth century, still continues and is remarkable for the birds' habit of nesting close to each other.

In modern times the Queen's right continues to be exercised in the practice known as 'swan-upping' on the River Thames. For a week in July or August, the Royal Swan-master and Masters of the Dyers and Vintners Companies and their crews, all in colourful dress, with large pennants flying, together make expeditions in fast rowing barges along London's river to capture and share equally all the young, non-pinioned swans. These birds are pinioned on one wing and released where they were caught.

Like most swans and some Mallards, the Coots and Moorhens of public places have learnt to lose some of their fear of Man and take advantage of our fondness for feeding any bird which will trust us to come close enough. The long-toed, red-billed Moorhen, with the white line along the side of its body and its nervously flicking white under-tail coverts, is more numerous than the Coot. This is a larger bird, lobe-footed and all black except for its white bill and shield on the forepart of its head which has given rise to the expression 'as bald as a Coot'.

The Water Rail is much less bold, except in a long period of severe frost when food is scarce, and it is difficult to spot in the well-vegetated wetlands where it lives a secretive existence. About two-thirds the size of a Moorhen, it is of two shades of brown and thinly built to enable it to move easily through closely growing marshland vegetation. Its presence is more often known from its calls, which vary from grunts and clicks to a more characteristic pig-like squeal, frequently uttered in spring. Very much rarer, less noisy

A family of Mute Swans is cornered on London's Thames by the Royal Swan-master and Masters of the Dyers and Vintners Companies. Each takes his turn to mark his own swans. 'Swan-upping', as this practice is called, was once widespread and dates back to the sixteenth century.

The Moorhen, more aptly and widely known as the Water Hen, is commonly found in every suitable habitat, large or small. In Britain's parklands it is becoming increasingly tame through people's love of feeding birds, as the Moorhen readily enjoys scraps.

and probably overlooked in many places is the smaller Spotted Crake. It has bred occasionally in densely grown marshes in many parts of Britain.

Green or blue above, according to the light, and reddish chestnut below, the Kingfisher is the most colourful of all our birds of marshes, lakes and rivers. Its numbers have been severely lessened from time to time by long periods of hard frosts, and a particularly large proportion of the population died during the bitter winter of 1962–3. Since then, a succession of mild winters has helped to restore its numbers and the birds are again widespread, though nowhere really common, throughout England, Wales and

One of Britain's most colourful birds, the Kingfisher, whose number suffered severely in the arctic conditions of the winter of 1962–3.

45

The male Bearded Tit whose British population was almost eliminated by persecution, severe winters and the destruction of its reed-bed habitat, is now numerous in the East Anglian marshes. From here it has spread to other sites in England as far north as Lancashire.

Ireland. In Scotland it is mainly confined to the south-west. The Kingfisher has also been helped by a decrease in river pollution so that more small fishes, like Bullheads, of which it eats a good many, are available. Both sexes, alike in their dazzling plumage, use their stout 1½-in. (40-mm) bills to dig a slightly rising nest tunnel some 2 ft (610 mm) deep into a river bank or occasionally in a sand-pit some hundreds of yards from water. Also brightly plumaged in many colours and with somewhat similar nesting behaviour is the Bee-eater, but this is one of the rarest birds ever known to have nested in Britain. A pair nested unsuccessfully near Edinburgh in 1920 and three pairs bred in a working gravel-pit near Lewes, Sussex, in 1955. Two of these pairs raised seven young, but the nest of the third pair was dug out before the identity and breeding activity of these most unusual birds was recognized and a guard placed on them by the RSPB.

Shaped like a big Wren, the dark brown, white-fronted Dipper is well named. Constantly bobbing up and down, it is to be found in rocky streams or lake sides, generally in hilly country, sometimes in low-lying areas. It is sedentary, strictly territorial and has the unusual ability to walk under water in search of food in its own stretch of water. Dippers breed over much of the British Isles but not in the northern isles nor in the south-eastern quarter of England. The Grey Wagtail is another, but very different, bird of the same habitat. The longest-tailed of our three members of the genus, it is gracefully slim, mainly blue-grey above and bright yellow below and inhabits a rather wider range of Britain's rivers and streams than the Dipper.

One of the most successful recoveries of a wetland species that humans and hard weather had almost destroyed is that of the Bearded Tit. Destruction of much of its specialized reed-bed habitat and collection for museums and for the decoration of Victorian hats and drawing-rooms had, by the turn of the century, reduced the population to only a few pairs. It is a most attractive little bird, mainly tawny orange, the male having Oriental side whiskers and a lavender-grey head. Protection was helping a build-up of numbers when the long spell of snow in 1947 killed off so many that only about ten were known in their last stronghold in Suffolk and Norfolk. But they are prolific breeders, having up to four broods in long, warm summers. Helped by good survival in a succession of mild winters and perhaps, also, by the arrival of some birds from Holland, as well as by a greater tendency to local migration and, especially, by the post-war development of new reed-beds, the population has now increased to some three hundred pairs, more than have been recorded in England for over 150 years.

Another partial migrant, the Reed Bunting, has long

46

shown itself less affected by hard winters, and good numbers are found throughout the British Isles, though only a few as yet have spread to Shetland. This plump, sturdy species, looking like a smart sparrow except that the male has a black head with a white collar in spring, is increasing everywhere. Its choice of habitat, which once confined it to marshland, is now being extended to dry areas.

Among the small marshland birds that survive by being wholly migratory are Reed Warblers, Marsh Warblers and Sedge Warblers. They are all 'little brown jobs' as American bird watchers, who are used to seeing brightly coloured warblers, call them. Mainly brownish, with pale underparts, only the Sedge Warbler has any distinctive streaking in its plumage. It is also more noticeable from its habit of making song flights in its territory and is by far the most abundant of these three, breeding throughout the British Isles except in Shetland. In contrast a similarly plumaged bird, the Moustached Warbler, has been known to breed here only once, at Cambridge in 1946. The Reed Warbler is common and breeds in England and adjoining Welsh counties while the Marsh Warbler, very similar in appearance, is rare: a small colony is found regularly only in Gloucester and Worcester and other evidence of nesting is found from time to time elsewhere in the southern half of England.

The Grasshopper Warbler is another small, rather nondescript summer resident of wetlands, breeding also, but less commonly, in dry areas of tangled, grassy undergrowth. Except when the male first arrives and has to advertise himself in his territory, the bird tries to stay out of sight and is often known to be present only by the sound of its remarkable reeling song which is like the noise made by an angler casting out his line. It breeds all over the British Isles in suitable habitats, unlike another small bird that has an almost similar song, the Savi's Warbler. This is another of those marshland species which disappeared from our country in the last century and which eventually returned to nest under protection in our new reed-beds. The first recolonization began at Stodmarsh, Kent, in 1960, then in Suffolk's coastal marshes ten years later.

The Nature Conservancy Council's reserve at Stodmarsh, near Canterbury, is a good place to see these wetland warblers and Bearded Tits and it is especially good for seeing one of England's newest colonizers, Cetti's Warbler. Since 1971 a colony of several pairs has developed here and breeding now also occurs in East Anglia. Unlike other warblers of our marshes this bird, more reddish-brown than a Reed Warbler, more skulking in its usual habitat of waterside brambles and bushes, does not migrate away from the country and its characteristically sudden burst of loud song may also be heard in the winter.

A Sedge Warbler with a full brood in a typical marshland site. In such places it can be identified by its prominent eye stripe. The male frequently indulges in a flight of song over its territory.

47

The Waders

Waders, as the name suggests, are birds which spend much time with their feet in water. The term includes the six British-breeding families of small to medium species, most of which feed and nest on the ground and are usually to be seen in flocks in the off-season, when they spend their time on sea-shores, estuaries and shallow, fresh water. Although much used by British birdwatchers the name is not wholly apt for a large widespread group of birds including as it does the plovers which feed mostly on sand, stones, mud and grassland, and the Stone Curlew, a bird of heaths and other dry places. The Americans call them 'shore birds' and use the term 'wader' for herons, ibises and other large, long-legged birds that do search in water for their food.

In past centuries in Britain, population of several wader species declined as the birds were taken for food. They were also affected by what is commercially termed wasteland being made suitable for agriculture and other industry. Such 'reclamation' is still found to be necessary in our highly populated country where now even once-remote beaches and estuary shores, vital nesting habitats for several kinds of waders, are over-run by people at leisure. However, with protection, about eight of our 20 wader species are increasing.

Most obvious and loud in voice and plumage is the Oystercatcher. Unlike its North American counterpart, this chunky black and white bird, despite its name, eats few oysters in this country where these shellfish are generally farmed in beds too deep for the birds to reach. Its diet does include cockles and mussels which it opens with its powerful, bright red bill and natural skill perfected by watching its parents when it was young. It also eats smaller molluscs, limpets, crabs and occasionally the eggs and young of other locally nesting birds like terns and Avocets. Unusually among waders, it takes food to its chicks, often from long distances. Oystercatchers nest on sand and shingle around almost all of the not-too-heavily disturbed sections of the coasts of the British Isles, extending inland in the north, and they are increasing.

Probably our best-known wader, because it is so common and widespread throughout the year, is the Lapwing,

The black and gold spangles of the upper part of the Golden Plover make it difficult to see on its nesting grounds in heather-covered moors.

OPPOSITE The Avocet had not nested in Britain for one hundred years until defensive flooding in parts of the East Anglian coast during the last war restored suitable conditions for them. About 150 pairs now breed in this area.

known also as the Peewit because of its very distinctive call. Seen on the ground it is a colourful bird, the dark green of the upper parts being shot with bronze and purple. Its long crest, short, sharp beak and the tips of the closed wings and tail give the bird a spiky appearance when standing but in the air its remarkably rounded wings make it appear more dumpy.

The Golden Plover, spangled on head, back and wings with black and gold, is also well named. In summer, British birds have blackish faces and breasts, which give them protective counter-shading when on their nesting grounds on heather-clad peat hags and moors. These birds breed most commonly throughout Scotland and on the Pennines but sparingly in widely scattered sites in Wales, Ireland and on Dartmoor. Winter flocks of several hundreds occur in favourite southern areas in low fields of grass or plough. A much rarer plover of the high moors of over 2,000 ft (610 m) in Scotland is the Dotterel. Its population is very low after many years of having its eggs stolen by collectors and of being shot because it was good to eat and its feathers made good flies for anglers. It used also to breed in good numbers in northern England but there it does so only rarely now. A pair recently bred in north Wales. Migrant flocks of hundreds which used to be seen at regular stop-over sites in Britain – several 'Dotterel Farms' can be found on Ordnance Survey maps – are now reduced to only small groups of half a dozen or so known as wisps. Like the phalaropes, the sexual roles of this colourful little wader are reversed: the more brightly chestnut-breasted female takes the lead in courtship and aggression and the male incubates the eggs and cares for the young.

Disturbance by people was a major cause of the disappearance, after 1956, of the Kentish Plover as a breeding bird of the British mainland. It is a worldwide species so its loss, sad enough, is only local and the birds may well return one day to breed on our shores. However, Man has been responsible for the establishment and widespread breeding of another small, related bird, the Little Ringed Plover. This species which, in Hertfordshire, first bred only as recently as 1938, takes advantage of the increasing number of water-holding gravel-pits and now numbers nearly five hundred pairs in England. Its range is also beginning to extend to Wales and Scotland. So far, very few pairs are nesting on sand and shingle banks in rivers as they commonly do on the Continent. In the breeding season the Little Ringed Plover is more active and noisy than its close relative the Ringed Plover, which breeds more commonly on our coastal beaches and in recent years has begun to spread to suitable sandy, dry and bare ground inland.

One of the most remarkable sounds to be heard from a wader in grassy marshland, especially on quiet days in late

A Snipe in the open shows its characteristic long bill and brown, buff and gold plumage. When disturbed from its usually well-hidden nest, the Snipe's zig-zag escape flight makes it very difficult to shoot at.

The Ringed Plover, a small bird, is just able to cover its clutch of four large eggs. Several pairs are known to breed inland but most nest on beaches.

BELOW It is not easy to find this Woodcock among the undergrowth because of its protectively coloured plumage.

spring and summer, is the so-called 'drumming' of the Snipe. It is made by the vibrating of the specially adapted outer feathers of the tail, which is spread at an angle of about 45° when the displaying male dives through the air. The sound is like the bleating of a sheep and lasts for about two seconds, coming to a crescendo as the dive reaches its maximum speed of some 35 mph (56 kph) or more. A female, when disturbed from a brood of young, can make a similar sound with her bill while standing on a near-by post or tussock. Snipe are also noted for their bursts of chippering calls, given from song-posts. Somewhat unusual for a wader, they frequently use a high perch on a dead tree, building, post and even occasionally on wires. The Snipe is a plump bird, very long billed and wonderfully coloured with stripes of golden and dark brown and cream. When disturbed it flies off with a recognizable zigzag flight, usually making a hoarse 'scaap' call which sounds as though it is more alarmed than it really may be. It nests in damp lowland meadows and high moorland bogs. It is a popular game bird throughout its wide range in the British Isles where it breeds in almost every county, most numerously in Ireland and Scotland. Its escape flight is so confusing that a skilled gunner is often known as 'a good Snipe shot'. Many birds from Scandinavia and other Baltic countries winter with us, birds from Iceland winter in Ireland, and are seen in small groups or 'wisps'.

Like the Snipe, the Woodcock relies a great deal on its light and dark brown plumage for camouflage. On its nest it is almost invisible to the human eye and no doubt also to most wild predators. Young birds are protected in the same way. Its long, straight bill, used for probing in the soft earth beneath the woodland carpet of fallen leaves, is held at a downward angle in flight which helps to make the bird recognizable. It is only occasionally flushed from the ground, most often by whistling and shouting lines of beaters on a game estate during a winter shoot, when it tries to escape by dodging in and out of the trees, but at first its flight is heavy and slow. Most people see a Woodcock in the breeding season, on its regular flight at dusk to a feeding ground or during its 'roding' display flight when, in the gloom, it patrols the boundaries of its territory. Like an owl, it flies quietly, but warning is given of its approach by its strange two-part call which is a high-pitched 'twissick' followed immediately by a low, grunting 'brr-brr'. Woodcock are mainly sedentary throughout their range in the British Isles and are joined by good numbers of winter visitors which arrive over the North Sea in late autumn, mainly, some people claim, under a full 'Woodcock moon' in November.

The 4–5-in. (100–150-mm)-bill of the Curlew is the longest of any British-breeding bird and is used to good effect in the soft sand and mud of shores and estuaries where it feeds. It also feeds a great deal on hard, dry ground, picking up insects and molluscs from the surface where the length of its legs balances the length of its bill, reducing the amount by which the body need be tilted. The Curlew used to nest mainly on high ground but now low valleys and moors are also used and nesting occurs in all counties except those around London and some parts of East Anglia. Named for its ringing call, this tall, brown bird with a white rump may be seen all the year round, unlike the similar, rather smaller Whimbrel, which is a summer visitor and much more scarce. Breeding regularly only in the Shetlands with a few spreading elsewhere in the mainland of north Scotland, its total population numbers only about two hundred pairs. It is, however, a fairly common migrant and may be seen in small groups or often singly, passing along our coasts in spring and autumn when it can generally be identified by its trilling call. It is less shy than the Curlew and may allow the birdwatcher a close approach to note the two broad, dark stripes on the head which make it recognizable.

Perhaps the most colourful of all our waders, the Black-tailed Godwit, is one of those wetland species we destroyed by marshland drainage and shooting in the last century. These high-standing birds with the long, straight bills, bold black and white wings and tails and red underparts in summer have, fortunately, been given the chance to make a come-back. Nesting began again in Scotland and East Anglia in 1937 and regular colonies are now developing, the largest being on the wet, grazed grassland of the Ouse Washes. Two pairs began to breed again in Suffolk in 1973 and others breed in scattered sites from Shetland to southern England. Many stop over on passage and more now spend the winter with us, feeding and roosting in flocks sometimes of several hundreds, mainly in East Anglia and the Channel counties.

The small Green Sandpiper, with dark olive-brown wings and back and distinctively white-rumped – and rather misnamed – has bred on one or two occasions in the north. A similar wader, the paler and more spotted Wood Sandpiper, is becoming established as a regular breeder in north Scotland where it was first known to nest in 1959. Both species occur as passage migrants and may be seen on muddy marshes, creeks, pond edges, sewage farms and other wetland areas where there is a good cover of vegetation. The Green Sandpiper is the more common and some spend the winter in Ireland and England. The Wood Sandpiper is so called because it prefers to nest in open wet patches in or by forests.

Much more numerous as a breeding bird, the Common Sandpiper is smaller, greyer and habitually flicks its tail up

A Curlew with one of its first-hatched chicks drying off its down. The Curlew has the longest bill of any British wader and this is used for probing deep in the mud for food. These birds do also feed on insects in hard, stony areas.

The Common Sandpiper, one of the more numerous waders, often adopts this pose in order to look for prey on the surface of the mud.

A Greenshank, nesting in the Scottish uplands, is removing the eggshell from which the last chick hatched. In more southerly parts of the British Isles, they are seen as spring and summer migrants whose identification is helped by their 'tu-tu-tu' call.

and down. It is a summer visitor, nesting on the ground close to water and is found throughout Scotland, northern England, most of Wales and Ireland and in scattered sites in some counties in the west and south. Also numerous is the Redshank, which breeds regularly throughout the four countries of the British Isles, except in the extreme south-west peninsulas of England and Wales, and is a partial migrant. It departs very early from its breeding grounds, as soon as the young can fly, and is found, with the addition of winter visitors from overseas, in varying numbers around our coasts. It is noted for its loud, ringing alarm call, especially when nesting, which causes it, in some parts of the country, to be called 'the warden of the marshes'. A high death-rate during the long, icy period of early 1963 occurred among many populations, which have only recently brought their numbers back to their normal average. These red-legged birds, which also have reddish, moderately long bills, can be identified in flight by their calls and by their broad white rumps and wing bars.

The Greenshank is somewhat similar but is larger and has dark wings and more white on the back. Its 'tu-tu-tu' call, uttered two to seven times together, is distinctive, and is similar only to that of the Yellowlegs, a very rare visitor from North America. The Greenshank may often be seen singly or in very small groups, though summer thunderstorms may force down migrating flocks of forty to sixty. In Britain it breeds only in north Scotland, in moorland where bogs and lochans are available, and one pair breeds in west Ireland.

Europe's smallest wader, the Temminck's Stint (only the Little Stint, from the Arctic, is almost as tiny, not much bigger than a sparrow), has occasionally nested in Britain. Between 1934 and 1951 single pairs were known to have nested three times in Scotland's Spey Valley and once in Yorkshire, the eggs failing to hatch in each case. A pair, however, at last managed to breed successfully, fledging three young, in another area of Scotland in 1971. Temminck's Stint is grey and more uniformly coloured than the commoner Little Stint, which we usually see as a young migrant in summer and autumn when its juvenile plumage is bold with black and buff mottling on the upper parts where two creamy lines form a distinct 'v' pointing towards the rump.

Like a larger version of the stints but with a black belly in spring plumage when it is also more brownish red on the back, the Dunlin is the most abundant and widespread of our birds of the shore and estuaries. Dunlins wheel in the sky in large flocks, sometimes mixed with other small waders, alternatively appearing dark then silvery as they show their top sides then their underparts. Because they are common and feed in company with other species, they are used as

Male Ruffs at a 'lek' where they show off their gaudy plumage to win the attention of the females. Once common, and slaughtered for food, the Ruff is now one of Britain's scarcer breeding birds.

yardsticks for the description of other rarer waders: an observer's field notes often starting with a phrase such as, 'Of the same shape and proportions as a Dunlin but …'. They breed over most of Scotland and the isles, sparingly in north, central and south-west England and in parts of Wales and south and west Ireland. They nest in high or low peat bogs and coastal saltings.

A welcome species to return to breed in Britain is the Ruff, which had ceased to breed in the last century. It was once common in England and popular as food for Man – trapped birds were fattened for the purpose on boiled wheat and bread and milk and sold for half-a-crown each. As they became scarce, more had to be imported, hundreds at a time cramped in baskets, from Holland. Many died on the journey. Poulterers continued to sell spring-caught Ruffs until late in the 1800s when, at last, the species was included in the bird protection laws which were slowly coming into being. Like so many other birds, they had also suffered from the drainage of wetlands. After some occasional breeding, mainly in Norfolk, a few pairs now nest regularly on the reserves in East Anglia's Ouse Washes where a nest was found in 1963, the first to be known in Britain since 1922. The plainly plumaged female, known as a Reeve, is much smaller than the male, which in spring is well known for its gaudy, backward-extended ear-tufts and ruff of feathers around its neck. Among individual males there is an extraordinary variety in this display plumage, which may be black, white, orange, brown, purple or buff, with or without bars, or a combination of two of these colours, the head plumes often being different from the ruff. This showy dress is not worn for many weeks but is used in the breeding season when the males gather together at a 'lek'. This is an open area used year after year when they give sudden bursts of display, plumes fanned, and attack each other in a lively manner – children used to be said to 'fight like Ruffs'. Sometimes an onlooking female will be impressed and excited enough to walk up to a male and invite mating, which might occur there and then, or the pair may walk off together, away from the crowd.

Two vagrant wader species have been recorded breeding only once in Britain. One, the Spotted Sandpiper, a pair of which were found nesting in Scotland in 1975, had come all the way from North America. The other was the Black-winged Stilt, whose normal range is around the Mediterranean and south-east Europe. Three pairs of these very long-legged black and white birds nested near Nottingham in 1945 and raised three young. No further attempts have since been made to breed in Britain.

Another elegant member of the stilt family, the Avocet, has, however, found suitable nesting conditions here in this century and there are two regular colonies in RSPB reserves in Suffolk. A few pairs also occasionally nest elsewhere. The Avocets once bred fairly commonly in eastern and southern England, but wetland drainage and persecution of the bird by Man, the combined cause of the disappearance of several of our species in the eighteenth and nineteenth centuries, caused it to stop breeding in about 1844. Two pairs bred only once in Ireland in 1938. Then, during the last war, when some coastal flatlands were flooded for defence and the public were not allowed to enter these areas, the Avocet made further attempts to breed. A pair probably bred in Norfolk in 1941, a pair was seen with chicks in Essex in 1944, then in 1947 four pairs were found nesting in a new habitat created by flooding at Minsmere in Suffolk and four or five pairs were also nesting at near-by Havergate, a flooded island in the River Alde. Each site quickly became an RSPB reserve, and the Havergate colony steadily increased to about one hundred pairs. The Minsmere birds, however, failed to nest when they returned in 1948 and did not do so again on that reserve until 1963 when the creation of the 'Scrape' was begun. This is a specially designed 50-acre (20-hectare) mere of shallow, brackish water, dotted with shingle islands and patches of mud, for the safe breeding of terns, waders and other species whose normal breeding sites on the coast and estuaries can no longer be used because of the growing activity of humans. Avocets are summer visitors – a small number winters in Devon and Cornwall – returning as early as mid-February if the weather is good, and they are seen more and more often around the low, coastal areas of England and Wales and at inland waters.

Last on the list of the true wetland waders which breed in Britain is the Red-necked Phalarope. It is one of only three species in the world of this unusual family in which, like the Dotterel, the role of the sexes is partly reversed. The female arrives first on the breeding grounds, establishes nesting territory, drives off other females, pursues the males when they arrive and takes the first step in courtship and mating. The male, less brightly plumaged than his mate, does all of the incubating of the eggs. Only small numbers of these phalaropes breed in the British Isles, in north Scotland and the northern and western isles and only recently they stopped breeding in western Ireland. Their nests have been robbed by unscrupulous egg-collectors for a long time but their decline may be due mostly to the climate. The Red-necked Phalarope is a summer visitor, occasionally seen on spring and autumn passage, just offshore or on small lakes or sewage-farms. A main, recognizable characteristic of this small, grey and white wader is that much of its feeding is done by swimming and rapidly turning round on the water to stir up crustaceans and insect larvae.

A female Red-necked Phalarope is unusual among birds in that she is more brightly coloured than her mate. A few pairs of this species breed in the northern isles of Scotland.

Birds of Mountain and Moorland

The oldest parts of the British Isles, the rocks which make our mountains, are in the west and north. Where the mountains meet the sea, their worn, crannied cliffs provide nest sites for several million sea birds. Inland, however, there are fewer birds on the bare tops and high, heather-clad slopes than are to be found in the varied, richer habitats of the lower parts of the country.

Our ancient peaks and cliffs are almost the last surfaces of Britain which have remained unaffected by Man. In lower inland hilly areas changes are being made at an increasing rate. Scattered quarries for slate, granite and other minerals have only a small effect on the bird-life but where there are soil-covered slopes, vast areas are being planted with trees. The Forestry Commission are covering the economically poor environment at the rate of 57,500 acres (23,000 hectares) per year and private plantings amount to only a little less. Most of the new trees are planted in Scotland and are of Sikta spruce which can withstand harsh weather conditions and low soil values, and only 2.5 per cent of the plantings made in 1975 were of broad-leaved trees.

The new woodlands have an enormous effect on the bird-life of mountains and moorlands where many species improve their populations by making the best use of the conifer plantations when they are young and relatively open and other species take advantage of them when they are older and densely grown. Herds of Red Deer which Man likes to see on heather tops and slopes affect birds' feeding and breeding by their control of vegetation, and keepers make a habit of burning moors to keep up the supply of young shoots for grouse and other game birds. In some places, carnivorous mammals like Foxes, Wild Cat, Polecat, and Marten are kept down for the benefit of game birds but not for the benefit of the birds of prey which need these animals for food and which are themselves persecuted by Man. Cereals, potatoes and other crops are grown in permanent or temporary sites that were once wet moorland or dry, gorse-covered heath, while other upland areas that were once cultivated are abandoned as uneconomic for food production in these modern times. These factors and the use of farm chemicals and drainage, the building of walls and

The magnificent Golden Eagle displays its strong, hook-tipped beak which is useful for tearing up prey like Blue Hares, found in the Golden Eagle's habitat of the Scottish mountains.

OPPOSITE The Raven shows its powerful beak. It is the largest of all Britain's crows and was once a common sight in London but now breeds on the remote cliff faces and mountains of the west and north of the country. Their nests are extremely large, as Ravens will return to the same nest throughout their lives.

This Hobby has just fed its chicks in a nest in a Scots pine. The photograph shows well its characteristic red thighs.

fences, and the greatly increased numbers of walkers, birdwatchers and other tourists are all having a noticeable effect on the bird-life of mountains and moorland. Some species can adapt to, or find suitable, these new conditions, but many cannot.

The White-tailed Eagle, also known as the Sea Eagle, is one species which Man eliminated completely from the British mountain scene, supposedly in the interests of his sheep. Once common around the rugged Scottish cliffs, it last bred in 1916 on Skye, where attempts at its reintroduction are now being made with young birds from Norway. Its main food is fish, sea ducks and gulls and carrion, and it does not compete seriously with the Golden Eagle which takes Foxes, Hares, other mammals and land birds. Protection by some landowners has helped the slightly smaller Golden Eagle, but not so much as it might, and this bird is still persecuted by keepers and egg-collectors. It also suffers when Rabbit populations are low through myxomatosis and through poisons acquired as a result of eating the carrion of sheep which had been passed through a chemical dip. Probably less than three hundred pairs now breed in the north and where possible the nest sites of this large bird – its wing span is up to 90 in. (2280 mm) – are kept secret.

Like a small eagle and characteristically broad-winged,

58

short-tailed and of patchy light and dark brown plumage, the Common Buzzard is much more numerous and is found over most of the western half of Britain. It has been and still is, illegally, much persecuted by Man but suffered its greatest set-back in this century in 1954 when its chief prey, the rabbit, was severely reduced by disease. Now both rabbits and the Buzzards are making a good recovery. The Kite is only very slowly making a come-back after being almost wiped out by Man and a lack of carrion. Once widespread and performing a useful service scavenging in the streets of London, where it bred until the late 1700s, its total population of less than thirty pairs is now confined to a few wild valleys in central Wales where the breeding sites in hillside woods are closely protected. Seen from below, as birds of prey most often are, it has longer and narrower wings than a Buzzard, large pale patches on the primary feathers, a reddish body and a long, pale red, deeply forked tail. As well as carrion, it eats small mammals, birds, frogs and worms.

A much better recovery is being achieved by the Hen Harrier, which also now enjoys a greater degree of protection. It breeds mainly in moorland in the northern half of Britain and in Ireland and Wales, finding more security, and food, among the newly planted conifers. The smaller Montagu's Harrier, a summer visitor which numbered some fifty to eighty pairs in the 1950s, has fared the worst of all our hawks and its population has completely crashed, none being known to have bred in Britain in 1976.

Our scarcest regularly breeding falcon, the Hobby, is also a summer visitor, about a hundred pairs nesting in the southern half of England and in Wales. It is a bird of low-altitude heaths and farmland with scattered woods where it may be seen dashing on long, dark, curved wings into a flock of birds. It can fly down a Swift with high speed and grace, or jink after a dragonfly or flying beetle. It is much less persecuted, except by egg-collectors, its clutch of three round eggs being particularly beautifully marked in one of a variety of shades of red from pink to brown, and laid in an old nest of another species, frequently a crow's. Perhaps twice as numerous and nesting only in the west and north of the British Isles, the Peregrine, our largest falcon, depends a great deal on protection. Because its food is mainly birds, which it strikes down in an incredibly fast dive, large numbers were killed during the war by orders of the Air Ministry who were afraid of losing carrier pigeons. A post-war recovery was followed by a short decline beginning in the mid-1950s when the deaths and failing ability to breed of many birds was said to be the result of certain agricultural chemicals whose use has now been discontinued. The Peregrine nests in lonely inland and coastal cliffs and is resident in its breeding range, and migrants from the

The Common Buzzard, whose prey consists largely of rabbits. When these animals were decimated by the disease myxomatosis the number of Common Buzzards declined severely.

A female Hen Harrier breaks up prey for its small chicks at their nest on an Orkney moor.

Continent are found occasionally in other parts. It is much admired by falconers, from whom its nests still require protection.

Our smallest falcon, the Merlin – $10\frac{1}{2}$–13 in. (270–330 mm) compared to the Peregrine's 15–19 in. (380–480 mm) – is also capable of astonishing speeds of well over 100 mph (160 kph). It too is in demand by falconers and on account of its size was known as the 'lady's hawk'; the peculiar name of the species comes from the Old English 'marlin', a name given generally to female birds used in hunting. It nests on the ground, or sometimes in the old nest of a crow or Magpie, and its present population of about five hundred pairs is spread over moors and open coasts in the north and west of the British Isles.

The slightly larger Kestrel, which breeds regularly throughout Britain and Ireland, except in Shetland, is less fussy in its choice of nest sites, using ledges on buildings in the centre of cities or on lonely sea cliffs, as well as haystacks or the old nests of crows in woodland. It is the most common and familiar of all our birds of prey, being seen characteristically hovering in many places, increasingly alongside motorways where in the grass margins it can see and pounce on small rodents. Despite persecution by gamekeepers of this most useful, and, with its chestnut upper parts, most colourful of our falcons, it has managed to maintain very good numbers.

The game birds of our wilder moorlands are found mostly in the hills of Scotland and northern England. The Red Grouse, a dark red subspecies of the Continental Willow Grouse and found only in the British Isles, has the widest range, breeding also throughout Ireland and in small numbers in Devon. It eats mainly shoots and seed heads of bell heather and ling, whereas the larger, less common Black Grouse, a bird of a different genus which prefers wooded heaths and bogs, eats the buds of trees like birch and a variety of seeds and fruit. Both have declined in this country though the Black Grouse rises and falls considerably in its numbers in Scotland and, in some areas of new afforestation, has increased. The Black Grouse, which has many mates, is well known for its habit of assembling at the special display grounds known as 'leks', where the lyre-tailed males make noisy displays to each other and to the duller-plumaged females, known as Greyhens.

Neither the Black nor the Red Grouse turns white in winter but the Ptarmigan, a relative of the Red Grouse, does. It is a bird of the high Scottish mountains and, like the white-winged Willow Grouse of the Continent, becomes protectively coloured among the snow-drifts in winter. With the Ptarmigan, up on a very few of these high tops, often in the Cairngorms, two to seven pairs of Snow Buntings arrive to breed in most summers. It is one of our

The male Kestrel displays. It is one of the most common falcons, nowadays frequently seen hovering over the short grass bordering motorways as it searches for food.

rarest breeding birds and the species which nests at the highest latitudes in the world – the Russians have recorded the bird at the North Pole. It occurs in good numbers in Britain only in the winter when flocks come down from northern Europe to feed in our coastal areas. Lower down the mountains, below the arctic zones, the huge, black-looking Capercaillie is found among the trees where it eats buds, especially of conifers and, when disturbed, flies off noisily like an airborne turkey. After becoming extinct, Continental stock was reintroduced into Scotland in 1837 and in later years and spread successfully, mainly within the central and eastern Highlands.

Two diurnal (that is, active during the day) owls live on our moors and other open spaces. One, the Snowy Owl, is our rarest regularly breeding bird. A single pair has nested annually in Shetland from 1967 to 1975 (only females were in the area in 1976). The other daytime hunter is the Short-eared Owl, which is found in good numbers in Scotland, northern England and north Wales, locally in coastal East Anglia and north Kent and occasionally elsewhere. Its numbers in each area are often affected by how many Short-tailed Voles, its chief prey, there are in that area. It also takes many birds, including adult terns which may be nesting near by. It is a brown-mottled owl with long-looking wings which it claps together beneath its body when an intruder is near its nest. Its 'ear-tufts' are only seen at close quarters.

At home in undisturbed areas between the shore and the tops of mountains in the wilder parts of the north and west, the Raven is the largest of our crows. Once a common sight in the streets of London, it has been much persecuted in the past two hundred years and is now rarely found in the south-east quarter of England, though it manages to keep up good numbers elsewhere. It has an unfortunate and unjust reputation as a killer of lambs and weakly sheep; it is in fact a great cleaner-up of carrion and kills Rabbits, Rats and other small mammals. It is one of the few bird species which mates for life and a pair will continuously occupy one site. The nest, on a cliff ledge, is massively built of sticks and grassy clods of earth.

The Chough is another of our crows which prefers to nest on cliffs, mostly at the coast. A resident, distinctive with a curved red bill, it too is not so numerous as it was and the present population of some seven hundred pairs is practically confined to the cliffs of Ireland, Wales, the Isle of Man and Argyll.

The Rock Dove, another bird of our coasts, is remarkable for seldom, if ever, perching on trees. The ancestors of our town and racing pigeons, and domesticated in Iraq as early as 4500 BC, pure-blooded Rock Doves now breed only in small numbers in parts of west Ireland, north-west

The Snowy Owl bred on a RSPB reserve in Shetland from 1967 to 1976. It is one of our rarest birds of prey.

A well-camouflaged female Ptarmigan on its nest, which is usually, situated on the high tops and rocky slopes of Scotland's mountains. The species changes its colour to white in winter to offer protection in snow-clad conditions.

Scotland and the isles, most wild stocks being interbred with birds of mixed ancestry. They nest in caves or crevices and look like the more familiar Stock Dove but are paler, have a white rump and two distinct lines of black on the inner wing.

The thrush of upland water-courses in steep, rocky gullies of the north and west is the Ring Ouzel. It is like a wilder, more dashing Blackbird with a crescent of white on the breast – more distinct in the male – and is a summer resident only. Smaller, open-country members of the big family of thrushes, the *Turdidae*, are the chats, the most common being the Wheatear. It is easily noticed by the prominent white basal half of the tail, a feature which gave rise to its strange name: 'wheatear' comes from Anglo-Saxon words for white rear. It is now far less abundant than it was, especially in England. On autumn migration it was so numerous on the Sussex Downs that it was recorded, in the *Linnaean Transactions*, that a shepherd caught eighty-four dozen in one day; around Eastbourne, the average annual catch in the early nineteenth century was about twenty-two thousand – many trappers caught these birds, which were regarded as table delicacies, in horsehair nooses set in vast numbers of shallow tunnels dug for the purpose all over the downs.

The Whinchat is also a summer visitor to our heathlands, and is found in the same areas and numbers as the Wheatear, but with many fewer in Ireland and a marked decrease in numbers in the south-east quarter of England. Stonechats are birds of rather similar habitat but are only partially migratory and their numbers are much affected by severe winter weather. It is important to all of these chats of the open country that they keep their habitat, which may be drastically affected by Man, grazing animals and fire. The widespread fires which occurred during the drought of 1976 caused severe drops in the populations of birds, reptiles, insects and rodents, and it will be several years before an ecological balance will be restored in many of the affected areas. Much concern is felt for the future of the Dartford Warbler, non-migratory and therefore already subject to population changes through hard weather. Breeding only on heather and gorse scrubland in central southern England, it was reduced to only about ten pairs by the severe conditions of early 1963 but had recovered to more than 140 pairs by 1971.

The Meadow Pipit was also affected by these heath and grassland fires, but this is an abundant species breeding throughout the whole of the British Isles in a wide variety of open areas. Its total number is more likely to be affected by Man's permanent destruction of its habitat as more and more rough land is cultivated. Such environmental changes, and those caused by grazing animals, also affect

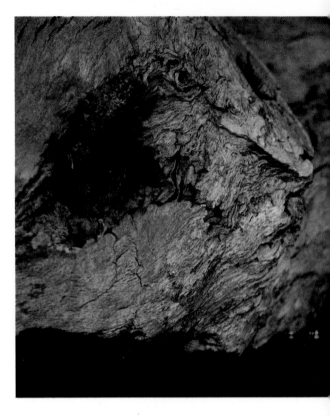

Wheatears usually build their nests in holes in the ground, walls or rocks but this female is taking food to a hole in a fallen tree. These summer visitors are not now so numerous in England as they were in the last century when they were trapped for food, but they still breed commonly in Scotland.

The Meadow Pipit, a bird which nests on the ground, is widespread throughout Britain. Some of its heathland territories were destroyed by fires during the exceptionally hot, dry summer of 1976.

A pair of Stone Curlews with one of their two newly hatched chicks, on a typical nesting site – Rabbit-grazed heathland. Because of the changing climate and the reduction in the Rabbit population the number of these birds has been greatly reduced.

the numbers of the Tree Pipit. A summer visitor, it breeds more commonly in the north and west and does not nest in Ireland. The larger, darker Rock Pipit is a bird of our coasts where it nests in most sections except south Yorkshire to east Kent and the flat coasts of Lancashire and Dumfries. It breeds and feeds among the rocks and cliff tops but occurs on sandy and muddy shores and marshes in winter.

Twites, small finches like dark, female Linnets, are also found on rocky coasts and cliff tops as well as hilly inland moors and around villages. They nest in north and west Scotland and Ireland and more recently were spreading in the Pennines, but there have been marked decreases in some populations. Outside the breeding season they move down from high land and flocks may be seen feeding around the coasts on plant-grown saltings.

Also decreasing in most of its habitat of heathy scrubland and woodland edges is the Nightjar. This moth-catcher, which is active at twilight when its strange churring song may be heard, is affected by the unwanted entrance into its breeding sites by people who might never see this secretive bird. Rank growth which developed while Rabbits were few is also a considerable disadvantage, but the bird is disappearing from some areas which still remain suitable. This may be due to climatic changes which affect vegetation, the quantity and variety of insect life and thus bird populations. The recent and sudden decline of the Red-backed Shrike may also be largely due to such changes. Once common and known as the 'butcher-bird' because of its habit of hanging surplus food like nestlings and beetles on thorns in a 'larder', it has disappeared from many of its old haunts and now breeds regularly in southern England and East Anglia only and in declining numbers.

The Stone Curlew, also aptly named Norfolk Plover and Thick-knee, is a somewhat mysterious bird whose weird, ringing call is heard much less often these days as the summer dusk falls over East Anglian brecks and southern downs. Resembling a small version of a species of bustard though not a member of that family, and remarkable for its large, staring, yellow eyes, it is now absent from many places where it was well known. A summer visitor, the groups it forms before emigrating, once of up to a hundred or more, are now on a much smaller scale if they occur at all at the favourite quiet heathland sites where they used to be seen each autumn. In Britain, it dislikes disturbance, but a few pairs continue to nest on ploughed land or woodland rides that, a few decades ago, were lightly grazed heaths. Until 1965, eight pairs used regularly to nest semi-colonially on a part of the shingle peninsula of Dungeness in Kent, but this area is no longer the great quiet desert of stones that it was and none does so now.

Sea Birds

The total surface area of all of the British Isles is not very large but their uneven shapes give them a very long coastline. We lie in a temperate corner of the ocean where the sea has been warmed by the North Atlantic Drift that has brought with it some of the heat from the Equator and the Caribbean. On Britain's Continental Shelf this water, highly salty as a result of evaporation, meets our fresher, river-diluted water and, where they mix, especially in areas between islands where the current is swift, make conditions which are excellent for marine life. Our birds do well. Lower forms of plankton are eaten by more developed kinds which are eaten by fishes and by birds – and birds also eat the fishes of manageable size.

Many sea-going birds, truly marine, use the land only for breeding. The success of their life-style depends on a safe nesting site where one chick, or no more than two or three, according to the species, can survive for a long period until it has developed sufficiently to be able to go out to sea. Unlike most land birds, it will have a long immaturity of three, four or five years before being able to obtain and hold a breeding territory of its own and, once it has matured, it will enjoy a longer life of twenty years or more.

The coasts of the British Isles provide a safe breeding site within reach of a good food supply, especially where our oldest rocks in north and west Scotland, Wales and Ireland stand as tall cliffs and stacks, weathered and scarred by the fierce Atlantic with many crevices and narrow ledges. Our sea-bird colonies are, therefore, very large and total some three million breeding pairs. As we have so many nesting birds, among which are the highest numbers of sea birds in Europe, our responsibilities are large. Nesting sites have to be protected, not-so-difficult a task where these are on cliffs but becoming nearly impossible where shores can be overrun by people. Conservationists also have to keep governments and industry continuously aware of the growing threat from the discharge of sewage, chemical waste and oil into the sea. A repetition of the large-scale destruction of sea birds and marine life such as occurred with the wrecking of the *Torrey Canyon* off the Scilly Isles on 18 March 1967 seems to be more probable with the increase

OPPOSITE Gulls are multiplying at an ever-increasing rate, partly because they are one type of bird which has little trouble finding food. The offal thrown overboard from this fishing boat is attracting Herring Gulls and Lesser Black-backed Gulls; these are young birds, as can be seen from the colour of their plumage.

in oil-tanker traffic into Europe, and offshore drilling. On that occasion, when a great many lessons were learned, 60,000 tons of crude oil spilled into the sea. Some ten thousand oiled sea birds were collected on the shores of the Western Approaches, nine out of ten of them being Guillemots, and uncounted numbers of these and other species died unseen. More deadly are the persistent organochlorine chemicals brought by rivers into our coastal waters, some from farms, some from manufacturing industries. But despite these threats and with the notable exception of three auk species and Roseate and Little Terns, most of our sea-bird colonies are increasing. The ancient custom of killing them in vast numbers and taking their eggs, for food, has virtually ended, as has shooting them merely for sport. Sea birds are also benefiting greatly from the increasing amounts of offal being thrown overboard by Europe's ravenous fishing fleets, but if the present rate of destruction of our inshore shoals is not strictly controlled by agreement within the European Economic Community, this advantage may gradually turn into a disaster.

One of the most recently successful of our breeding sea birds is the Fulmar. Now numbering some 100,000 pairs and nesting on nearly all of our cliffs, though still very sparingly in the south-east quarter of England and rarely on low sections of the coast, it is difficult to imagine that it was as recently as 1878 when our only colony was on St Kilda, a lonely rock west of the Hebrides. Ornithologists are divided in their opinion as to the reasons for the sudden increase in the numbers of British and Irish Fulmars, for this success is not being matched by the western Atlantic populations of the species. It has been linked to the increased amounts of offal from fishing and whaling but another theory does not associate the population explosion with Man: it considers it might be due to a spread of breeding range being aided by the recent gradual increase in temperature over a wider area of the seas around our coast. Fulmars are like thick-necked gulls but are patchily grey above and, a main difference from that family, they have nostrils which lie in tubes along their upper mandibles. In flight, they do not show the typical gull-wing outline but glide very frequently, on stiff, straight wings, flapping only occasionally. A sitting bird on a rock ledge or grassy cliff top can defend itself by spitting a jet of oil at an intruder – this may be on an innocent sheep who will thereafter carry a highly unpleasant smell on its wool.

The Manx Shearwater is another 'tube-nose' of moderate size. It may be three times as numerous as the Fulmar, but nesting as it does in holes in the turf of rocky slopes and cliff tops and coming ashore only after dark, its numbers are extremely difficult to estimate. It is very open to attack on land because the special build of its body for swimming makes it a poor walker, and it is frequently taken by Greater Black-backed Gulls, whose trade-mark is to leave the Shearwater's skin turned inside out. It breeds at scattered places on the cliffs and islands of Ireland and the western seaboard from the Scillies to Shetland, returning in 1967 to the Calf of Man after 150 years' absence. There is only one chick, which is deserted when about three months old, and bloated with food it waits in its burrow for another two weeks before venturing into the sea. Large flocks may follow migrating shoals of sardines. Over their feeding sites, the nearly well-named Shearwaters glide on stiff wings, often at an angle just above the surface, the wing tips always just missing the surface. As they tip from side to side the birds appear black then white as they show first their upper then their undersides. One of the largest colonies is on Skokholm and Skomer Islands off South Wales, where Ronald Lockley, an authority on the species, and others have marked many thousands by putting numbered rings on their legs. It was a surprise when it was learned that these birds winter off the coasts of Brazil and Argentina, where many are shot.

Our smallest sea birds are the petrels, so called because they appear to walk on the water, like St Peter, before they alight on it. The name was used as early as 1703 by William Dampier, the English buccaneer who piloted the expedition which rescued Alexander Selkirk (Robinson Crusoe). Another name used by sailors for these tiny sea birds was Mother Carey's Chickens, perhaps because they suggested little black imps accompanying a legendary sea witch or perhaps from 'Madre Cara', to whom Italian sailors offered prayers at the beginning of a gale. Two species of petrel breed in the British Isles: the 6-in. (150-mm)-long Storm Petrel in large numbers in holes at scattered sites along the western coasts and islands up to Shetland, and the slightly bigger, less numerous Leach's Petrel, which is known only on four remote small islands of north-west Scotland. Dark, with white rumps, they are like larger, maritime House Martins, but only come ashore to nest, when the single egg is placed in a hole in which the sitting birds of both species croon continuously. Leach's Petrel is not often seen; unlike the Storm Petrel it does not follow ships at sea.

In contrast, the very large Gannet, which measures 36 in. (915 mm) from bill tip to tail, is often seen at sea or at one of its sixteen breeding sites on islands off the Scottish mainland, south Wales, southern Ireland or the Channel Isles. It frequently moves along the coasts at any time of year, though it is seldom in northern waters in the winter. Adult plumage is not grown until the birds are five years old or more, and it is mainly white with black wing tips and buffy head and neck. Juveniles start off appearing to be

LEFT This photograph of a Manx Shearwater was taken by flashlight after dark, the only time when these birds can move around on land, as they are ungainly out of water and easy prey in daylight for predatory gulls.

A pair of Cormorants preen their plumage after fishing, and one hangs its wings out to dry.

almost black but whatever stage of pied plumage in between that of the young and adult bird they may have reached, they may be easily recognized at sea by their pointed cigar-shaped bodies and very long wings on which they glide frequently, seldom very high above the surface. To catch their fish, Gannets dive from up to 100 ft (30 m) high in the air, entering the water with a spectacular splash and closing their half-opened wings just in time.

Two other sea birds which depend on fish are our Cormorant and Shag. Each looks large and black, the former near the size of a Gannet, the Shag some 6 in. (150 mm) smaller over all and having a shaggy crest in spring. It has no white on the face and flanks like the Cormorant and is an oily greenish black, whereas its relative, at close quarters, can be seen to reflect bluish tints in its more brownish-black plumage. Both species are present all the year and breed all round our coasts except between the Humber and the Solent. The breeding population of Shags is about four times that of Cormorants but they are much more maritime (that is, they prefer to be at sea) and are less often seen beyond their breeding sites in the season. They both stand upright, the Cormorant often being seen with its wings 'held out to dry'.

Skuas are mainly dark, gull-like pirates which roam the seas pursuing terns until they drop the fish they are carrying, or harrying gulls until they disgorge what they have swallowed. They are summer visitors to the British Isles where two species, the Arctic Skua and the Great Skua (also known as the Bonxie) breed, but only in Shetland, Orkney, some of Scotland's western isles and northern coastal areas. The Great Skua is like a large, heavy-bodied, immature gull, dark brown all over but with a distinctive white patch on the wing. More than three thousand pairs nest, three times the number of the smaller, more gracefully built Arctic Skua. Both species are famous for the ferocity of their power dives upon an intruder – man, sheep or other animal – into their nesting area. Although it is so much the more numerous, the Great Skua is the least frequently seen of the two when they are on passage round our coasts, generally being farther out to sea.

It is hard to imagine that our most bold and abundant scavenging sea bird, the Black-headed Gull, was a rare visitor to London up to the early 1890s. Now ever present and well known, this gull has greatly increased its numbers, finding a variety of food in our growing wasteful activities and becoming an important predator of pest insects on every piece of plough and stubble. In parks and gardens it has learnt to make good use of our affection for other birds, swooping in to snatch food we offer the smaller species. Both male and female are alike and have dark chocolate facial masks in summer. They breed on most parts of our

A Black-headed Gull regurgitates food for its large, begging youngster. It has become one of the most common species of gull, feeding on man's waste and on the food provided by increasing agricultural activities.

68

low-lying coast where they are not constantly bothered by Man. They prefer to keep company with others of their species and colonies are large, reaching ten thousand or more pairs if left undisturbed. In a large colony which has been developing during this century on the Hampshire coast, a few Mediterranean Gulls, larger, with black hoods and no black on the wing tips, have also bred since 1968.

The Common Gull is far from being common in the breeding season outside its nesting range in the Scottish Highlands and coasts and in north and west Ireland. A few pairs nest at Dungeness in Kent, and only here and there elsewhere in England. At other times, it is as frequently seen on rubbish dumps and following the plough as is the Black-headed Gull, from which it can be distinguished by its larger size, black ends to the wings narrowly tipped with white and greenish-yellow bill and legs. It has a white head, but the Black-headed Gull's head is also mainly white in off-season plumage.

The Herring Gull is of similar appearance but is still larger, with a heavier, fierce-looking bill, and is one of the most numerous of our gulls. It is found at all our coastal towns, especially at fishing ports. It breeds in scattered colonies on most shores, on steep cliffs, rocks, beaches or dunes, but few of them breed between Flamborough Head and north Kent. Closely related but with a grey back and wings and yellow, instead of pink, legs in adults of the British race, the Lesser Black-backed Gull is much less abundant over approximately the same range. It is mainly a summer resident, migrating to Iberia and north-west Africa, but an increasing number is wintering in England and Wales. This gull scavenges less than the Herring Gull,

The graceful, apparently effortless flight of the Herring Gull, which soars above every seaside town and breeds in abundance around the coasts of the British Isles.

An Arctic Skua, alighting at its nest in northern Scotland, shows the characteristic white flash on its wing. Skuas are pirates, forcing other sea birds to disgorge food which they have caught.

but both species prey often upon other breeding neighbours, especially terns and waders.

Our largest gull, the Great Black-backed Gull, is an even more greedy predator upon colonies of smaller sea birds. It also takes Rabbits and any other animal it can pounce upon and kill with its powerful bill. At sea it also feeds a great deal on waste discarded from fishing fleets, and the current abundance of such food is probably the chief reason for the bird's great increase in population. From very small numbers in the last century it has grown to several thousand pairs, nesting in colonies, though seldom large ones, on the coast of the British Isles except in east and south-east England.

With some half million pairs nesting on the cliffs all round our coast, the Kittiwake is now our most abundant gull. Its population is rapidly growing at a similar rate to that of the Fulmar and it is having to find extra living space on man-made cliffs like buildings in sea-side towns. Its food, almost entirely of small fish, especially Sand-eels, crustacea and offal from fishing-boats, is still in plentiful supply and large feeding flocks may be seen offshore. The Kittiwake, named from the call uttered constantly in its crowded breeding colonies, is like a Common Gull, a little smaller and with jet-black wing tips. Immature birds have a zigzag pattern of dark brown across the wings and may then be confused only with young Little Gulls. This, Europe's smallest gull, only 11 in. (280 mm) long, is seen much more rarely. A pair laid

eggs on an RSPB reserve, in the Ouse Washes, on the Cambridge/Norfolk border in 1975 but one bird was killed and they did not hatch.

Five species of sea terns breed in Britain. They are all summer visitors and are recognizably different from gulls in the way they feed – they all catch fish or shrimps by plunging from the air, an act of skill only rather poorly copied at times by the Kittiwake. All have slim bodies, grey backs and wings and deeply forked tails, and are told apart mainly by their size, colour of the bill and legs and their different calls. They are also unlike most sea birds in that they do not seek the safety of cliff ledges and holes and, nesting on open beaches, dunes or low, rocky islets, are much more likely to be disturbed by Man. One species, the Little Tern, which prefers to nest close to the sea, has had so many of its sites made unsuitable by people that its population in Britain and Ireland has been reduced to only about 1,800 pairs, making it one of our rarest sea birds.

Populations of our largest and whitest tern, the Sandwich Tern, named after the bay in Kent from which the first specimen to be described was taken in 1787, now total some thirteen thousand pairs. This is a large increase since the beginning of this century, and although colonies do not use their coastal sites regularly, their success has been greatly helped by human protection: many colonies are on reserves. These black-billed terns nest in closely packed, almost slum-like conditions, always noisy and quarrelsome, and the site is strong-smelling from the birds' droppings and the remains of uneaten fish, generally Sand-eels. The Gull-billed Tern, a similar species seen very rarely in Britain, has bred here once, in 1950, on an Essex reservoir. It has a shorter, thicker bill and feeds mainly on insects which it captures by swooping or when walking.

The other three of our sea-tern species are all similar to each other in size and each has red legs. The Roseate Tern, with a short-lived, hardly noticeable pink flush on its breast in spring, is the whitest-looking of these three and it has a longish, mainly black bill. It is one of our rarest breeding sea birds – population has recently fallen to fewer than 1,500 pairs nesting in a very few sites, usually small, rocky islands, round the coasts of the British Isles, mostly in Ireland. It is so like the other two terns that it was only discovered to be a species in its own right in 1812 when a specimen was shot on the coast of Bute by a Dr McDougall – hence the bird's scientific name of *Sterna dougallii*.

The Common Tern, which breeds all round the low coasts of the British Isles except in south Wales and south-west England, and at a few inland sites, appears to be less common than it was. It is about half as numerous as the very similar Arctic Tern whose colonies, mainly on the coasts of Scotland, Ireland and western England, total some forty

The Kittiwake, Britain's most common gull, is so called because the air around its sea-cliff breeding colonies is filled with cries of 'Kitti-w-a-ak'. So numerous are they that some have had to resort to finding nesting sites on buildings at the seaside.

LEFT A male Common Tern displays to its sitting mate and shows the black-tipped red bill which distinguishes it from other tern species.

Razorbills, one of Britain's four breeding auk species, are very numerous on rocky coasts in the north and west. They lay their single eggs in the crevices of sea cliffs.

thousand pairs. Away from their breeding sites, these two species are difficult to identify separately. The Common Tern has a black tip to its red bill; the Arctic has a shorter, dark red bill, greyer body and, when standing, its coral-red legs can be seen to be very short. Their double call-notes, 'kee yaaah', often used when they are nervous or afraid, are similar, though an experienced ear can hear the stress placed on the first syllable by the Common Tern. Seen in flight on migration, they are so alike that birdwatchers are often able to record them only as 'comic terns'.

Although the Black Tern is mainly a marshland breeder, it is most often seen in Britain as a migrant offshore, or on coastal pools where its dipping method of feeding off the surface in flight shows that it belongs to a different genus from our sea terns. The species bred regularly in east and south-east England until the mid-1800s, then a few pairs have bred again, in East Anglia, since 1966, but with small success. As a first breeding record for that country, a pair raised a chick in Ireland in 1967.

In the British Isles we now have four species of auk (the name stems from the Old Norse *alka*, given to various sea birds). They look like the flightless penguins of the Southern Hemisphere, with their white fronts and black backs, standing nearly upright, but they can fly well enough, under water as well as in the air. One member of this family of Alcids, the Great Auk, could not fly and so was eventually killed off by hungry seamen. In Britain, it was last known to have nested on St Kilda. Auks breed in colonies on the north and west coasts and islands, though none nest on the mainly unsuitable coast between south Yorkshire and eastern Hampshire. Of the four, the Guillemot is the most numerous of our sea birds, with a total population assessed by the BTO at more than half a million pairs. It nests in thousands on the faces of high cliffs, making counting difficult, but where this has been possible figures suggest the population is falling in the southern part of its range. The same thing is happening to the numbers of the Razorbill, in total less than a quarter as numerous as the Guillemot, among which it frequently nests, though it prefers crevices, holes and rocky shores. Its single egg is laid in a safer situation than that of the Guillemot and is less pointed at the narrow end, not needing that protective shape which prevents it rolling off narrow ledges. The Black Guillemot, more fond of nesting in holes, also has a more rounded egg. It is smaller than the other two, the only auk with a patch of white on the wing, and it has remarkably bright red legs and feet.

The Puffin also has reddish legs but its outstanding feature is its triangular bill, colourfully banded with blue-grey, red and yellow in summer. The basal part of this unique bill is shed after the breeding season, leaving it less grotesquely large for a bird which stands only 8 in. (200 mm) high. Puffins, difficult to count at their lonely breeding sites on western and northern coasts, have been estimated at totalling about half a million pairs, a much smaller number than there were a hundred years ago. Their name probably came about because the chick looks like a little puff of down. Alone, the young bird spends seven weeks at the end of a tunnel, generally a rabbit burrow at a cliff top, where it feeds on small fish brought in by the parents. The Sand-eels, Sprats and small fry, five to ten at a time, are carried crosswise in the bill by the adults. They do not feed their chick in the last week so that hunger forces it to the entrance of its hole and, waiting there until dark to avoid predatory gulls, it walks to a take-off edge and launches itself down to the sea. It will be many months before it sets foot on land again.

The Black Tern is one of the group of marsh terns and feeds by dipping gracefully to the water to take food from the surface.

A Puffin with a beak full of Sand-eels. The colourful sheath of its bill is lost after the breeding season when most birds spend their time out at sea.

Birds of Woods, Farms and Gardens

In the Late Stone Age, about 2400 BC, Neolithic Man crossed a Strait of Dover narrower than it is today and brought his completely new method of farming to Britain. He found the country mostly covered by a forest of oak, elm, lime and thorn, with alder on the marshes and waterlogged valleys and beech on the well-drained chalk and limestone. This density and variety of woodland, providing shelter for many kinds of birds, had been reached after a series of periods in which hazel and Scots pine had been the chief species. Before that, Britain had been covered by conifers which followed the birch woods, which, in turn, as the last glaciation moved back northwards between ten and fifteen thousand years ago, had themselves developed from the mossy tundra of scattered birch and willow, struggling to live in the track left by the plantless ice-sheet.

At first, with tools chipped from flints which they mined with antler picks, the new farmers cleared parts of the more open downland forest to grow the seed and breed the domestic animals they had brought. Then, as the Bronze and Iron Ages followed each other, they invented more efficient tools and the forest began to be changed more quickly into cultivated and grazing land. By the time of the Normans, so much woodland had been cleared that King William found it necessary to set aside some of the remaining areas as royal forests where deer and other animals, including birds, could be preserved for hunting. Still surviving today as Britain's first nature reserve, the best known of these is the 66,000-acre (26,700-hectare) New Forest in Hampshire.

As the vegetational cover of Britain was changed by the climate and, comparatively recently, by the more rapidly effective hand of Man, so the number and variety of our birds has changed. Up in the extreme north and north-west, the climate was growing gentler and allowed Wrens and Starlings to colonize islands and, as isolated populations, develop such individual characteristics as to qualify as subspecies. Some Scots pine-wood birds, like the tiny Goldcrest, managed to survive in remaining areas of their habitat then were able to spread out again as new plantations of exotic conifers were made. Others, like the

OPPOSITE A male Blackbird removes a dropping from its nest of large young. It is hard to imagine that this friendly bird, which will even come right into a house to take food, was once wild and wary and remained mainly in woodland edges. The breaking up of forests which occurred with the change in the use of land in Britain led to the expansion of this species' habitat and it adapted remarkably well. Blackbirds have also profited from the kindness and affection shown to birds by the British.

giant Capercaillie, became rare, were finally killed off by sportsmen and had to be reintroduced.

Wetland was drained to allow the growing of more crops and trees, thus drastically changing the local variety of birds, and lessening the numbers of those which were dependent upon aquatic vegetation. Insect-eaters of many species were affected by the changing number of trees, especially of oak, which is the richest provider of invertebrate food for birds. When woodland clearances had been made, regrowth was prevented by grazing animals, particularly Rabbits, which had been introduced by the Normans, sheep, which were more and more widely farmed by thirteenth-century Cistercian monks; and goats. Pastures and grazed commons developed where trees and bushes had covered the land, providing habitat for Wheatears instead of Wood Warblers and causing other dramatic changes in the bird-life. Soon, open-range sheep-walks had to give way to a system of enclosures which had to become more widespread to meet the needs of the expanding eighteenth century. Thousands of miles of new hedgerows were made. Basically of hawthorn but here and there with oak and ash and, especially, the 'immemorial' English elm (currently being slaughtered by a beetle-borne fungus), they sheltered other useful plants like blackberry and nettle and, by extending the habitat of birds of woodland edge and copse, helped these species a great deal.

Men who liked hawking took young from the nests of many falcons. Then, as large estates became common, predatory birds of all kinds were ruthlessly slaughtered in the almost-religious belief that the fewer their number, the better it was for game birds. But these estates, with their protected parklands and coverts, together with the many more cultivated gardens in town as well as country, produced more fruits, flowers and new soil surfaces which helped other species.

The clearing of our forests to about a tenth of their extent of four thousand years ago had an especially serious effect upon the numbers of our short-winged bird-hawks that had remained safe by being able to dash around and between the trees. As well as having its numbers reduced by the loss of habitat and by human persecution, the Sparrowhawk, which takes all kinds of small birds and a few small rodents, was also badly affected by farm chemicals which many of its prey had absorbed and which collected in its body until they reached a deadly poisonous level.

Now that use of the more dangerous pesticides has been banned and the bird has been protected, since 1962, by law, the Sparrowhawk population is increasing and it is found in most of the British Isles. Its bigger relative, the Goshawk, is now rare and breeds only occasionally in widely scattered sites, mainly in the north. The Honey Buzzard is rarer still and its few breeding sites between the north and south of Great Britain are kept secret. It is a summer visitor and likes the grubs of bees and wasps and also eats lizards, small mammals and birds which it can obtain on the ground.

The game birds for whom many of our birds of prey were sacrificed included the Red-legged Partridge (introduced from the Continent in about 1770), the English or Grey Partridge (a native), the Quail (a summer visitor, now rare) and the abundant Pheasant (probably introduced by the Normans). All birds of prey are now protected by law in Britain, but this has *not* caused a fall in the numbers of game birds. Partridges, the migrant Quail and the very few Bobwhite Quail, introduced from North America, have all suffered rather more from the increased use on farms of machines and chemicals. Our colder springs have also been harmful to these birds, as has been the increased use of the countryside by the public and their dogs. The continuing clearance of hedgerows and the tidying-up of the small plants at their base are other important man-made disadvantages for these as well as other birds. The Corncrake, once widespread, especially in fields left for hay, where its rasping call made its presence known, has become rare in the last hundred years, mainly through the mechanization and growing frequency of grass-cutting. It is able to maintain good numbers only in parts of Ireland, north and west Scotland and the isles.

In contrast, modern farming, especially the increased growing of cereals, has been of considerable benefit to most of Britain's doves. The Woodpigeon, the largest, was also helped by finding more areas for shelter and nesting in the new conifer plantations and by the growing of green crops on which it could feed in winter. Its population reached pest proportions over much of the British Isles but it has shown some reduction in the last decade. Also resident but less abundant, the Stock Dove, too, spread and multiplied but declined sharply from about the late 1950s, apparently partly from eating seed dressed with organochlorine pesticide. This blue-grey dove breeds in holes in trees and rocks, often in rabbit holes. It is smaller than the Woodpigeon and does not have that bird's white patches on the neck and wings, nor does it have the white rump patch of the Rock Dove, which lives mostly on sea cliffs in the remote north-west.

A fourth member of our resident dove family, the Collared Dove, has undertaken a most remarkably rapid and thorough colonization of Europe, spreading from the Balkans to the North Sea in twenty years. Entering the British Isles in 1955, when its first-ever nesting caused great excitement, it spread very quickly across the whole country, even going on to breed in Iceland. It is now so numerous in many areas, especially around gardens and chicken-runs, as

The Collared Dove has made a remarkably rapid extension of its range from south-east Europe. First arriving in 1955, it now breeds over most of Britain and is resident.

A young Cuckoo, only one or two days old, ejects the eggs from its foster parent Tree Pipit's nest. From now on it will receive all the food brought to the nest by the adult Tree Pipits.

A huge young Cuckoo is fed by the Reed Warbler in whose nest it was hatched. Reed Warblers are often found fostering a young Cuckoo.

to be unpopular and disliked by some for its noisy calling in the very early hours of dawn in summer. The similar Turtle Dove is a wilder migrant with a more pleasant, crooning 'turr turr'. It breeds mostly in the lowlands of England and the Welsh borders and only scarcely in Scotland and Ireland.

The Cuckoo, with its voice which is unique (but easily imitated by humans) and a double reputation as a herald of spring and a destroyer of family life, is known by name to all but would be recognized in the field by few people other than experienced birdwatchers. It breeds throughout the British Isles but is less common than it was until only a quarter-century ago. In level flight it is like a grey Kestrel but with noticeably shallow wing beats. The female has a loud, bubbling call and is parasitic upon about fifty species, especially the Hedgesparrow (Dunnock), Meadow Pipit, Robin and Reed Warbler. Her eggs, of which she may lay more than a dozen all in one area in a short season, are often fairly well matched to those of the foster-parents. One is laid in each nest, an egg of the owner being removed and eaten at the time. When the young Cuckoo hatches twelve days later, it instinctively wriggles the other small young or eggs on to its back, one at a time and pushes them out over the side of the nest. It is a very slow and tiring task for the blind and naked chick but is an essential part of its survival because it will quickly grow much bigger than its foster-parents and will need all of the food they can gather.

The breaking-up of our forests and the establishment of farmland, parks and hedgerows dotted with old, tall trees was at first of benefit to our woodland owls, but changing farming practices and human persecution soon caused the numbers of some species to fall. The widespread Barn Owl, which nests in hollow trees as well as old buildings, and the Long-eared Owl, which uses the deserted nests of other birds and prefers fir woods, are both more efficient killers of rats and mice than Man is. Their big ears and eyes, which fill a large area of their skulls, and the ability to turn their heads through $270°$ make them excellent hunters. Each species is distributed over much of the British Isles, though the ghostly white Barn Owl is more likely to be seen, especially at dusk and occasionally in full daylight, than the truly nocturnal Long-eared Owl.

The Tawny Owl is very much a bird of the night and seldom seen but is well known for its 't'wit t'woooo' song, much loved on tape by stage and radio producers. It is our most common owl, almost as much at home in a line of trees in a city street as in quiet woods or churchyards. The Little Owl, an unwise and unnecessary introduction from the Continent in the late 1800s, spread quickly over England and Wales but its numbers have now fallen a great deal. It

The Tawny Owl is the most common of British owls and is generally active only after dark when its well-known 't'wit t'woooo' call can be heard in tree-lined city streets as well as in bleak country churchyards.

likes more open country, and although only 8 in. (200 mm) long it can kill and carry prey as big as Blackbirds and Common Terns.

The woodlands, parks and lanes of Great Britain (but not of Ireland) provide a living for four members of the woodpecker family. The Green Woodpecker, which does not breed in north Scotland, is the largest and spends much time on the ground feeding on ants which it captures with its very long, sticky-tipped tongue. The Great Spotted Woodpecker, most widespread and recently increasing, and the tiny Lesser Spotted Woodpecker, which breeds only in England and Wales, feed in the trees. All three are resident and are helped through the winter by being able to feed on insect larvae which they dig, lick or spear out of the trunks and branches. The Wryneck does not look very much like the typical woodpecker: it has a long, soft tail and is wonderfully camouflaged in grey and brown. It has a short beak and does not dig out its own nest hole like the others, but it does have a long, sticky-tipped tongue which it uses for picking insects not only out of bark but also from leaf litter and sand-dune vegetation. It is named for a remarkable ability to twist and turn back its head. A migrant, arriving in early spring, it was once common in south-east England and was also seen in northern counties and in Wales. It now breeds rarely, if at all, in those countries, but began to colonize Inverness-shire in 1969, it is thought from Scandinavian stock.

A brightly coloured Green Woodpecker approaches its nest hole which it would have excavated with its mate. The stiff tail acts as a necessary support against the tree.

79

A Swallow returns to its nest in an old watermill. It is a welcome arrival in Britain in the spring having travelled some 6,000 miles (9600 km) from winter quarters in South Africa.

The Woodlark was also once more widely known in England, and in Wales, but is now rather scarce. A bird of tree-dotted scrub, it is only partially migratory. The fall in its numbers is recent and thought mainly to be due to climatic changes. The Skylark, however, continues to be numerous and is probably our most widely distributed bird. The resident population of between two and four million pairs is joined by large numbers from the Continent which winter here.

Our only species which are probably entirely insectivorous are the Swift and the three hirundines – Swallow, House Martin and Sand Martin. While Sand

Martins need more open country with water and banks to dig nest holes in, all are found around small towns and villages in good number throughout the British Isles in spring and summer, the fewest being found in north-west Scotland and the isles. The large, almost all-black Swifts are here for the shortest time, arriving at the end of April, and few stay beyond the end of September. Sand Martins do not stay much later, but Swallows and House Martins may be seen in our currently mild late autumns, some occasionally during November and even until early December. They spend the winter in Africa, the Swallow going as far as the Cape.

Somewhat owl-like, the 'hoo-hoo-hoo' courtship call of the Hoopoe is rarely heard in Britain, where one or two pairs nest very occasionally in holes, generally in trees, in southern counties. Several birds which have wandered over from the Continent may be seen in spring, however. They look exotic and are easily recognized by their boldly barred black and white wings and tail, pink-brown body, curved bill and large crest which is frequently fanned out. Another rare breeding bird which is highly distinctive in call and plumage is the Golden Oriole. The brilliantly yellow and black male and the greenish female are, however, very difficult to see, for the birds are secretive in mature woods or rather dense alder carr (fenland wood, i.e. a damp area) or poplars. They are more often heard than seen – the male may be heard calling teasingly 'I'm-an-*Ori*ole' from high up in the foliage, against the light. They are widely distributed on the Continent except in the north, but in Britain there is only one small, regular colony in East Anglia, though breeding occurs occasionally in other south-eastern counties. An exception is the pair which bred in Fife in 1974.

The various members of our crow family, although they are not aware of it, help to keep down the numbers of our small birds. Jackdaws, Jays and Magpies are well known as robbers of eggs and nestlings. Each is keeping up good populations in the British Isles except in eastern England, where the punitive action of gamekeepers is having a noticeable effect. Carrion Crows are especially persistent in taking the entire clutch or brood of ground-nesting birds like ducks or waders. Where colonies of gulls, even as big as Herring Gulls, provide a surplus of food, these crows may take away eggs and bury them with uncracked shells, in scattered sites, so that they can uncover and eat them. Jays commonly bury acorns and beech mast, successfully spreading the trees (when the seedlings are not grazed by rabbits and other animals) because they often forget where they have put the seeds. The grey-bodied Hooded Crow is found in Ireland and also in Scotland where it hybridizes with the Carrion Crow. Both are more often seen as singles

The Jay, most colourful of Britain's crows, steals the eggs and young of many small birds. It also spreads the growth of oak trees by forgetting where it has buried acorns, one of its main foods.

A Skylark at its nest in a typical location in grassland. No longer eaten by humans and taking advantage of increased agriculture, it is now one of Britain's most numerous small birds.

A pair of Rooks at their nest, part of a noisy colony. Unlike Carrion Crows, Rooks lead a communal life and feed in flocks in fields and stubbles.

or pairs, unlike the sociable Rook, which is well known for nesting in noisy colonies, most picturesquely in elms around old churches. Rooks feed in flocks in pastures, stubbles and ploughed fields; they have a diet which is more vegetarian than the other members of their family, the *Corvidae*.

The busiest and most entertainingly gymnastic of all our birds of woods, farms and gardens are the tits. One species, the Crested Tit, is found only in central northern Scotland where its specialized habitat of old Scots pine forests provides suitable nest holes in decaying trees. The Coal Tit is also a lover of pines but is widespread throughout the British Isles, and in Scotland it is the dominant tit in woods of all kinds. Like the more colourful Great and Blue Tits, it is easily attracted to food placed near houses in winter. The rather sombre Marsh and Willow Tits may also come to gardens. Neither breeds in Ireland, nor in Scotland much above the border, and neither is suitably named. The Willow Tit shows only a slight preference for marshland fringes. It may be told from the very similar-looking Marsh Tit by its nasal 'chay chay' call and, at close quarters, by its dull, instead of shiny, black cap. Feeding flocks of several species of these woodland tits may be seen outside the breeding season, making noisy and bustling progress along a lane or woodland edge. Often with them will be a dozen or more Long-tailed Tits. Tiny-bodied and weighing about a third of an ounce (10 gm), this restless pink, black and white bird whose 3-in. (75-mm) tail is longer than its body is not a member of the true, hole-nesting tit family. It is sometimes called the Bottle Tit because of the shape of its nest, which is woven from moss and cobwebs and incorporates from one to two and a half thousand small feathers, and may be found in a thorn bush or a fork in a tree.

Tree-creepers also join these foraging flocks, mostly feeding very differently by making rapid, jerky progress up the tree-trunks, probing with their long, curved bills for insects in the bark; they use their stiff-quilled tails for support, like woodpeckers.

Even more active on the trunks and limbs of trees, being able to move sideways or head-first downwards quite as well as upwards, is the Nuthatch. Hardly bigger than a plump, short-tailed sparrow but more colourful, it is well named, and it uses its powerful beak to hammer open hazel nuts, acorns and beech mast which it has lodged into a crevice. It is a sedentary bird, found mostly in Wales and the southern half of England. The Wren is able to make itself at home almost anywhere and with ten million pairs spread over the whole of the British Isles, in all kinds of environments from the storm-swept rocks of St Kilda to London's parks, it is one of our most abundant species. With its stumpy tail it is shorter even than the Goldcrest, but more plump, and it compensates for its lack of size by much use of its very loud voice.

Many people consider our best songster is the Blackbird. By good fortune, but more because of its ability to make the best of the change from a mainly wooded Britain to a country that is mainly farmland with hedges and copses, it is also one of our most common birds, being scarce only on open moorland and mountains. A shy forest creature up to only about two hundred years ago, there is now scarcely a garden which does not have one, and some are so tame that they will even enter the kitchen. The Song Thrush, well named even though it monotonously 'sings its song twice over', is almost equally widely spread but is less numerous. The largest of the family, the Mistle Thrush, is still less common, though it is found in most parts of the country except the isles of the north and north-west. It is the storm cock which sings loudly from the tops of bare trees on windy days in the winter and early spring, and though it appears to be wild and unwilling to trust in Man it will often nest in a tree in a garden. As its name implies, mistletoe is one of the many berries and fruits it eats.

These three thrushes are resident and can be seen almost anywhere. A fourth, the Ring Ouzel, is a bird of mountain and moorland and has been mentioned in the appropriate chapter. It is a summer migrant and behaves in the opposite way to what we expect of another of its relatives, the Fieldfare, which comes to us in the winter. Remarkably, a pair of Fieldfares raised young in Orkney in 1967, and since then these birds, spreading their range from the Continent, have bred in several places on the Scottish mainland and in the north and Midlands of England. The Redwing, another northern thrush which visits Britain in large numbers in the winter, has also extended its range and small numbers have bred in Scotland since 1925.

With the characteristic proud-chested, upright stance of the large family of thrushes, the *Turdidae*, to which it belongs, the Redstart is one of the most colourful small birds of our woodland edges and parkland. It is a summer visitor, nesting in holes in trees, sometimes in quiet buildings and garden sheds and occurs in most of Britain, highest numbers being in the west and north, fewest in the south-east. It is named for its nervously flicking red tail. A relative, the Black Redstart, is one of our newer colonizers, and was first known to breed regularly only in 1923. It is fairly fussy about where it likes to live, choosing ruins and large buildings like power stations, and probably less than a hundred pairs arrive each year to breed in central, eastern and south-eastern England. All too many suitable sites were provided for it by the bombing of London and Dover during the Second World War.

The Blue Tit is a friendly but cautious bird and a popular visitor to town and country gardens, attracted by food which kindly humans put out for it. One of Britain's most acrobatic birds, the Blue Tit is as colourful as any imported cage bird.

The male Redstart, a colourful small bird of the woods and lanes. This nesting site, a natural hole, is a typical one for this species but they will also use sheds in country gardens.

Several of our birds have been made famous by writers and composers and are well known to people with even the smallest knowledge of ornithology. The Nightingale, which nests only in small numbers north of the Humber–Severn line, is known by name to all though few would recognize one if they saw it. It is dull reddish brown above, with a red tail like a Redstart, but is bigger – 6½ in. (165 mm) long. Some claim its song has been romantically overpraised. It sings as much by day as after dark, but hearing its strong, pure notes on a still, spring night, when other birds are quiet, leaves one with little wonder that for more than two thousand years poets have been compelled to sing its praises.

The Robin is even better known. It is our national bird, resident throughout the British Isles except in Shetland, and even though it is only half as numerous it is much more to the fore than the Wren. The tameness of the Robin is proverbial and endearing and it gives much pleasure to many people in this country by being easily persuaded to eat out of one's hand and by being a useful companion to a gardener. Continental Robins are much wilder and migrants from the north and east which pass through Britain can be told by their lack of confidence in humans as well as, in the case of the more distant races, by the paler colour of their red breasts. We used to name the bird from this, the most outstanding feature of its plumage, but 'Robin', a shortened form of the French 'Robert', has gradually taken over as a pet name for our most-loved bird.

Except for the rare Dartford and Cetti's Warblers,

The Goldcrest, five of which make an ounce, is one of Europe's two smallest birds; the other is the Firecrest. The British population of Goldcrests was severely reduced by the hard winters of 1947 and 1962–3.

LEFT A pair of Blackcaps at the nest – the female has a brown head. This species is widespread and migrates to tropical Africa though a small but increasing number winter in Britain and Ireland.

RIGHT This male Pied Flycatcher has just caught an insect and will now return to its nest, probably in a hole of a tree, to feed its young. This particular bird has been ringed in order that its migratory habits and other behaviour can be studied.

Britain's fifteen species of warblers ,are summer visitors. They are all slim, thin-billed, mainly insectivorous small birds and may be roughly grouped according to their feeding habitat of marshes, trees or bushes. Of the latter kind, the Dartford Warbler can only be found in a few southern areas of gorse and heather, a habitat that was much reduced by the heath fires of the hot summer of 1976. Four others of this genus, *Sylvia*, the Blackcap, Garden Warbler, Whitethroat and Lesser Whitethroat, are fairly numerous except in north-west Scotland and the isles, but the latter species does not breed in Ireland and in only a very few places in Scotland.

Of our leaf warblers, so called because they feed a good deal in the trees (but nest on the ground), the Willow Warbler is the most widespread. It is well known for its delicate song, a liquid, descending trill. The very similar Chiffchaff, mostly identified from the song after which it is named, is also common, but not in north and east Scotland and the isles. The Wood Warbler is the least common of all of this group, being more fussy in needing a woodland habitat with a thick canopy of trees and, because of the shade, less ground cover. Although, like the related Willow Warbler and Chiffchaff, its plumage is mainly an unnoticeable olive-green with some yellow on the breast, it is rather larger and brighter and its song is known for having two phases, one a trill which reaches a shivering crescendo, the other a repeated, very liquid 'peu' note, much like a Nightingale.

Of similar behaviour are our, and Europe's, two smallest birds, the Goldcrest and the Firecrest. Each weighs about a fifth of an ounce (6 gm), but the Goldcrest is, on average, very slightly shorter and is widespread throughout Britain and Ireland. The bright red on the head of the Firecrest, a few of which have been known to breed in southern England only since 1962, is hidden under its yellow crown stripe, like the Goldcrest, and is only shown in display. It is different from its close relative by being generally of brighter plumage and having a distinctive black and white pattern to the side of the head. The plain-faced Goldcrest looks wide-eyed and always surprised. Both are resident and locally migratory in Britain and like to join feeding flocks of tits. Many, especially Goldcrests, are seen on passage to and from the Continent in March and April, and again in October.

Remarkably enough, we have only two breeding flycatchers, small migrants which live in trees, short-legged because they frequently perch and seldom walk and broad-beaked because they catch insects in flight. Apart from their feeding habits, they are very different from one another. The Pied Flycatcher is black and white, nests in holes and is found in wild parts of Wales, the west and north of England

A male Pied Wagtail. The most friendly of Britain's three wagtail species, it will often breed around houses as well as in wetland.

and parts of Scotland. The Spotted Flycatcher is larger, grey-brown above with grey streaks (not spots) on its breast and is common and widespread throughout the British Isles, except Shetland. It is a friendly bird, nesting in a tree fork, a garden shed or in the roses round the cottage door. Both species are summer visitors only, for they have to return to tropical Africa to find their insect food in the winter.

The Hedgesparrow, equally well named as the Dunnock, is found almost everywhere and is far more common than may be supposed. It is not easily noticed with its dun-grey and brown plumage, and because it creeps around the bottom of bushes and among lesser plants, finding insects in summer and seeds in winter. Its loud, warbling song is not to be ignored, however, being quite like a Wren's but not so harsh and heard during most of the year. It is sedentary and much used by the Cuckoo as a foster-parent.

Wagtails could hardly have been given any other name – not that it has been the British practice to be particularly apt in naming a bird after its most obvious characteristic. The longest-tailed, the Grey, is a bird of fast-running streams, while the Pied and Yellow are more likely to be found on farmland and meadows. The Pied Wagtail is a resident, found throughout the country, while the Yellow is a summer visitor, scarce in the north and west of the British Isles. Pied Wagtails are the least afraid of people, coming readily to scraps put out in the garden, and in winter they will sometimes roost in large numbers inside buildings, entering through skylights. Nottingham's postal sorting office, brightly lit and very busy all night, was a popular site at one time.

Of all the town-roosting birds which have learnt to overcome their fear of Man and take advantage of the warmth to be found in a city in winter, the Starling is the most widely disliked for this practice and for the mess it makes – guano (bird-droppings) is only useful if it gathers in one place, like the famous sea-bird islands off the coast of Peru which produce enormous quantities of fertilizer. As well as the ten million or more Starlings which are resident in Britain, several million come to us for the winter from the Continent. The birds do very well, of course, on food which we waste or kindly provide them, but the main reasons for their enormous population growth in the past 150 years are probably increased agriculture and the fact that the climate has grown gentler.

Most of our finches, too, have benefited from the expansion of our farming, especially the growing of cereals. The Greenfinch and the Bullfinch are widespread and numerous, except in the northern isles, and as well as taking advantage of orchard and seed crops and weeds which are found among them, they have become at home, all the year

86

LEFT A cock Linnet at its nest. The nest would have been built by the female, no doubt encouraged by the male's song and company.

This male Bullfinch is about to bathe. It is an increasingly common bird except in the far north of the British Isles.

round, in both town and country gardens. Even more abundant and now one of our most frequently seen small birds, having recovered from a general decrease about twenty years ago, the Chaffinch is much liked for its cheerful 'pink pink' call and the beauty of its nest, neatly made with wool, moss, spiders' webs and fine roots and grasses and decorated with lichens. The Goldfinch is also well known, except beyond the Scottish border country, and has made a very welcome increase in post-war years now that the law and public opinion have virtually put an end to the very cruel practice of capturing and caging wild birds. The Linnet has also benefited from the same change in public behaviour, though in some areas a rise in local populations was reversed by the changing of its favourite habitat of gorse-covered scrub into farmland. It is well known for its cheerful, if not powerful, song. A male Linnet sings a great deal, especially as he accompanies his mate while she does all the work of nest-building. The crimson of his forehead and breast become brightest during the long breeding season when the brownish tips to the feathers are worn off.

Like small Linnets but having black chins, Redpolls are

A male Goldfinch 'stopped' in flight by high-speed flash photograph. A numerous species, these birds are often to be found in suburban gardens.

87

fussy, busy little finches with a distinctive buzzing call in flight. They are increasingly common in most parts of the country, having been helped by the continually spreading plantations of our Forestry Commission, whose woodlands now cover more than 9,000,000 hectares. Siskins, equally small finches but mainly black and yellow, have especially benefited from this work. Their main stronghold is Scotland, where they were once dependent upon the native forests of Scots pine, but now they are colonizing new plantations of exotic conifers in all parts of the British Isles. Curiously enough, they have taken to feeding on peanuts put out in gardens in hanging plastic-netting bags for other finches and tits.

Europe's smallest finch, the Serin, is also yellow with some black streaks like the Siskin but it is related to the Canary and has the stubbier bill of birds of that genus. Following a northward spread across Europe in the past two hundred years, a pair of Serins eventually bred in England, in Dorset, in 1967, but very little breeding has occurred in southern England since then. At the other end of Britain, a new finch to breed was the Brambling, which nested in Sutherland in 1920 and may later have done so in a few other places in Scotland and in England. It is the northern relative of the Chaffinch, recognized mainly by its white rump and dark head, and sometimes very large flocks from the Continent winter here, their movements varying according to the state of the weather and the availability of stubbles, beech mast and weeds.

Finches depend on seeds for much of the year, the different sizes eaten by the different species requiring a range of strong beaks. Our biggest finch, the Hawfinch, has a diet which also includes stones of fruit like cherries and to cope with these its beak is an enormous cone and it has large jaw muscles in a big head, giving the 6½-in. (165-mm) bird a bull-necked appearance. It is a secretive, chestnut and buff bird of woodland and shrubby gardens, seldom heard singing, even in spring, and is not often noticed in the areas where it can be found, mostly in the south-eastern quarter and the Midlands of England. Our other finch with a very heavy bill is the Crossbill. Its uniquely crossed mandibles, used in a scissor action, enable it to open pine cones, its chief food. Males are brick-red, females green and immatures streaked greyish green. They are usually unafraid of people and are best seen in the places where they are most numerous – the pine forests of Scotland and East Anglia; their diet makes them thirsty and they can often be watched at Forestry Commission water-tanks.

Buntings are like our big family of finches: they have the same strong, short beaks for seed-eating but they occur more on the ground, often in open country. The largest, the Corn Bunting, is different from the other members of the

This Corn Bunting chick is being overfed because it is one of only two young. These birds usually produce four or five chicks in a brood.

family in that both sexes are exactly alike in plumage, which is rather dull brown, and its outer tail feathers are not white. The males have more than one mate and being thus kept busy with territorial affairs, leave the nest-building, incubation, and feeding of the young to their females. They are resident over the eastern half of Britain, mostly near the coast, and outside the breeding season roost with others of their species in long grass. To make their cheerful, if monotonous, song, which has been likened to the jangling of a bunch of keys, the males like to perch on telegraph wires in open country. Song-perches are so important that local populations may desert an area if the Post Office takes down its lines and puts them underground.

The brilliant Yellowhammer is as vividly coloured around the head and underparts as a Canary, but it has none of that bird's attractive notes. Its song, a single repeated phrase, is well known as 'A-little-bit-of-bread and no che-e-e-se'. It is resident, very common and widely distributed, unlike the Cirl Bunting, which is similar in appearance but with a black throat in the male and is found only in the south-west and central southern half of England.

It used to be said that some Londoners had difficulty in recognizing a House Sparrow when they saw one in the country as the birds were so different in plumage that was not dulled by smoke. The Clean Air Acts have long since done away with the chance of such an unfortunate difference and the sparrow is immediately recognizable everywhere for what he is, a bright chestnut, black and grey bird which can make the best of any situation, entertainingly bold but very wary – and very numerous. Profiting from the free food and warmth provided by the way we now live, House Sparrows, and Starlings for some of the same reasons, are among our most abundant species. So closely connected with Man are they that when some inhabited islands have been deserted, the House Sparrows have removed themselves as well. The House Sparrow looks like a finch or bunting, but is a member of the big group of weavers which has many representatives in Africa, where they commonly hang bamboos and village trees with a community of their nests. Our House Sparrows nest mainly in buildings, but they occasionally nest in a group in thorn bushes near houses. Our other weaver, the Tree Sparrow, is much less numerous, wilder, less fond of humans and likes to nest in holes in trees, sometimes in buildings and nest boxes. It may also build in other, larger bird's nests, not necessarily deserted ones: in one of the few trees near an isolated farm on Dungeness, Kent, recently, a Carrion Crow's nest containing four large young had the nest of a House Sparrow, also containing young, woven into one side while on the opposite underside a pair of Tree Sparrows had their nest and eggs.

A male Cirl Bunting courting his mate by feeding her on the nest. The distinctive black and yellow throat of this species can be seen clearly.

89

5 Winter Visitors and Passage Migrants

Since the last war, and more clearly as equipment has improved, radar has shown that there is no time of year when migrant birds are not journeying across or within Britain. Daytime movements are also noted down by a growing army of watchers at coastal bird observatories and other favoured points.

Of the two hundred or so species which breed here, about one-third winter over a vast area from France to the tip of South Africa; some sea birds spend the whole of the off-season out in the Atlantic. Their return takes place from mid-February to late May, and they and their young leave again between early July and mid-November. In addition to these millions of our own birds, moving in flocks or singly at different times over most of the year, vast numbers come regularly from elsewhere in north-west Europe to spend the winter here or to rest and feed *en route* to or from other winter quarters. And from the northernmost island of Shetland down to the Scillies, Britain acts as a long-stop for passage migrants blown off-course towards a watery grave in the ocean by severe easterly gales. From the opposite direction come smaller numbers of New World birds. These are migrants which, beginning their autumn journey from the northern Continent to Central or South America, are caught by strong westerlies blowing across their coastal fly-way and manage to survive the long Atlantic downwind flight. Some will have had a partly assisted passage on boats but will, in any case, be near exhaustion and will need to spend several days or weeks here, recovering their strength.

In spring, some south-west European species may overshoot to Britain on their northward migration from Africa, and if our weather happens to be nearly as suitable for them as that of their native northern Mediterranean lands they may stay and wander here for many weeks. Young gulls of several species scatter in all directions to spend their first years away from their home sites. Many other immature birds, especially of those families of waders and birds of prey which do not breed in their first year, make a non-urgent, dry-run migration towards the areas of their birth in the far north or north-east of Europe where they will nest in a future year. They include some of the same species as ours, but are larger and sturdier races and they occur in Britain when our own birds already have eggs or young.

Every few years there come from the north-east particularly large numbers of specialist-feeding birds like Crossbills, which eat seeds in pine cones, and Waxwings, which eat berries and fruit. We receive a share of these flocks which, when a highly successful breeding season is followed by a poor food crop, are forced to spread south and west in search of better stocked areas. Crossbills are very early breeders and groups of old and young may begin to

Greylag Geese, part of a large number which winter in south-west Scotland having arrived from their breeding quarters in Iceland.

PREVIOUS PAGES Migrant Oystercatchers (black and white), Redshanks and a lone Knot (smaller and greyer) roost at high tide while their feeding area is covered.

arrive from across the North Sea in early June. Waxwings do not burst forth until later and we see them in force in late autumn or, sometimes, not until midwinter. Large numbers of other birds also come here irregularly in search of food. They are weather migrants, hardy species of sea birds, waterfowl, waders, larks, finches or buntings which are forced to move when their northerly or north-easterly feeding areas become frozen or covered in snow.

Britain's maritime climate is, generally throughout the year, mild and moist, more so in the mountainous west and north, where the Gulf Stream has its main effect, than in the low-lying east which sometimes comes under the influence of Continental extremes of summer and winter weather. The surface of our land, as varied as anywhere in the world, is not for long under snow or ice and it is small wonder that many birds from farther afield in north-west Europe depend for their survival on wintering here. They are mainly birds with a vegetarian diet or those which can feed in our coastal or river-estuary mud.

Roosting Swallows, photographed at dawn in Central Africa, where they have paused on their way to winter in the southernmost part of that continent.

93

Many sea birds, with a diet of fish, molluscs and crustaceans, spend their off-season in our coastal waters. They include the divers, Red-throated and Black-throated, and sometimes the Great Northern from Iceland and Greenland. Grebes like our offshore waters too, including those of our four breeding species as well as the Red-necked from the Continent. Fulmars, Gannets, Razorbills and Guillemots can also be seen from the coast, especially when fish shoals come close, but Puffins generally spend the winter farther out to sea.

Among the diving ducks to be seen at sea from time to time are Scaup, generally in small numbers. Common Scoters may occur in large groups which occasionally include some of the rarer Velvet Scoters, identifiable by white wing patches. The still rarer Surf Scoter, from North America, has white patches on the head and none on the wing. Eiders, breeding more numerously round our northern coasts, Iceland and north-west Europe, are more often seen in our southern waters in winter. The King Eider, the male of which has a peculiar peaked forehead, is a very scarce visitor to the east coast from islands round the Arctic. Red-breasted Mergansers, in small numbers, fish in bays and estuaries and come less often to reservoirs or other freshwater pools than the related Goosander or the small and rarer Smew.

The largest birds to come to us for the winter are the Whooper Swans from Iceland and the far north of the Continent. They like to feed in bays and lakes, mostly in the north, whereas the smaller, more musical Bewick's Swan from Siberia grazes the fields and flooded meadows of the south, especially on the Severn and East Anglia's washes. Geese find Britain much to their liking when they have finished breeding and moulting in the far north. Flocks of Greylags arrive in Scotland, Ireland and northern England and others pass through the east and south to winter elsewhere. Whitefronts, of the race which breeds in Greenland, winter in Ireland and west Scotland; those from Arctic Russia, paler and with a pink (not yellow or orange) bill, winter elsewhere in Britain, especially in the south-west. Bean Geese, darker than the Greylags, also come from the north and east, and they find their best feeding in East Anglia and south-west Scotland. The smallest of the grey geese, the Pink-footed, comes from as far afield as north-east Greenland, as well as Iceland, and feeds in our stubbles, meadows and potato fields.

Our one resident 'black' goose, the Canada, is joined in the winter by two others of the *Branta* genus. ('Brant', or 'Brent', is from the Anglo-Saxon word for burnt, describing the charred or blackened appearance of the necks of these birds.) The little Brent Goose, the only one whose head is all black, comes in large numbers from the Arctic and feeds on

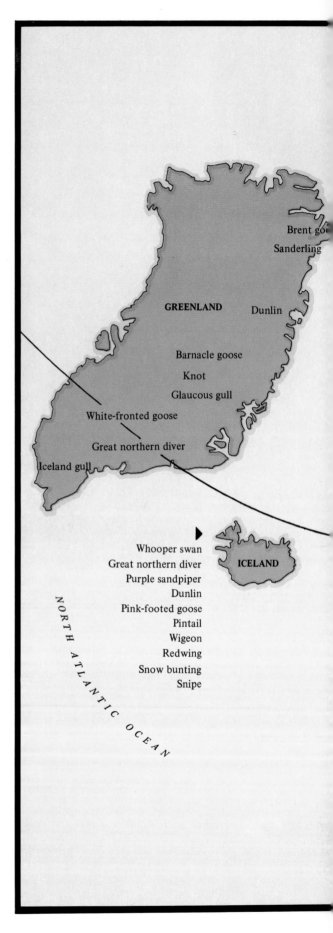

GREENLAND

Brent go[ose]

Sanderling

Dunlin

Barnacle goose

Knot

Glaucous gull

White-fronted goose

Great northern diver

Iceland gull

Whooper swan
Great northern diver
Purple sandpiper
Dunlin
Pink-footed goose
Pintail
Wigeon
Redwing
Snow bunting
Snipe

ICELAND

NORTH ATLANTIC OCEAN

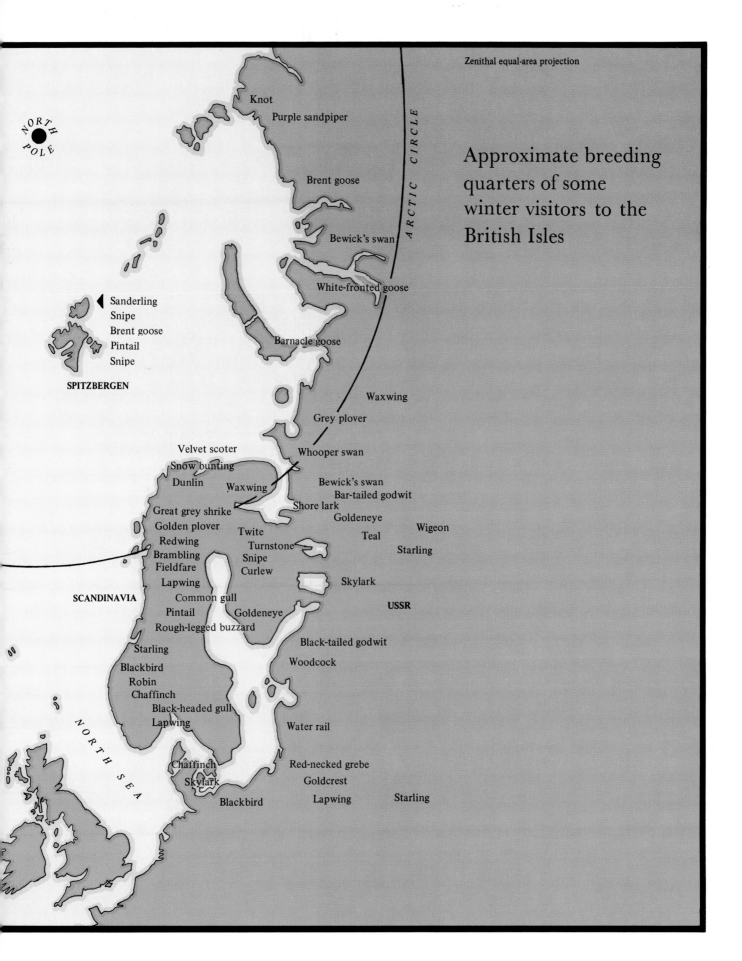

Zenithal equal-area projection

Approximate breeding quarters of some winter visitors to the British Isles

NORTH POLE

ARCTIC CIRCLE

Knot
Purple sandpiper
Brent goose
Bewick's swan
White-fronted goose
Barnacle goose

Sanderling
Snipe
Brent goose
Pintail
Snipe

SPITZBERGEN

Waxwing
Grey plover
Whooper swan

Velvet scoter
Snow bunting
Dunlin
Waxwing
Bewick's swan
Bar-tailed godwit
Shore lark
Great grey shrike
Goldeneye
Golden plover
Wigeon
Redwing
Twite
Teal
Starling
Brambling
Turnstone
Fieldfare
Snipe
Lapwing
Curlew
Common gull
Skylark
Pintail
Goldeneye
USSR
Rough-legged buzzard
SCANDINAVIA
Black-tailed godwit
Starling
Woodcock
Blackbird
Robin
Chaffinch
Black-headed gull
Lapwing
Water rail
Chaffinch
Red-necked grebe
Skylark
Goldcrest
Blackbird
Lapwing
Starling

NORTH SEA

95

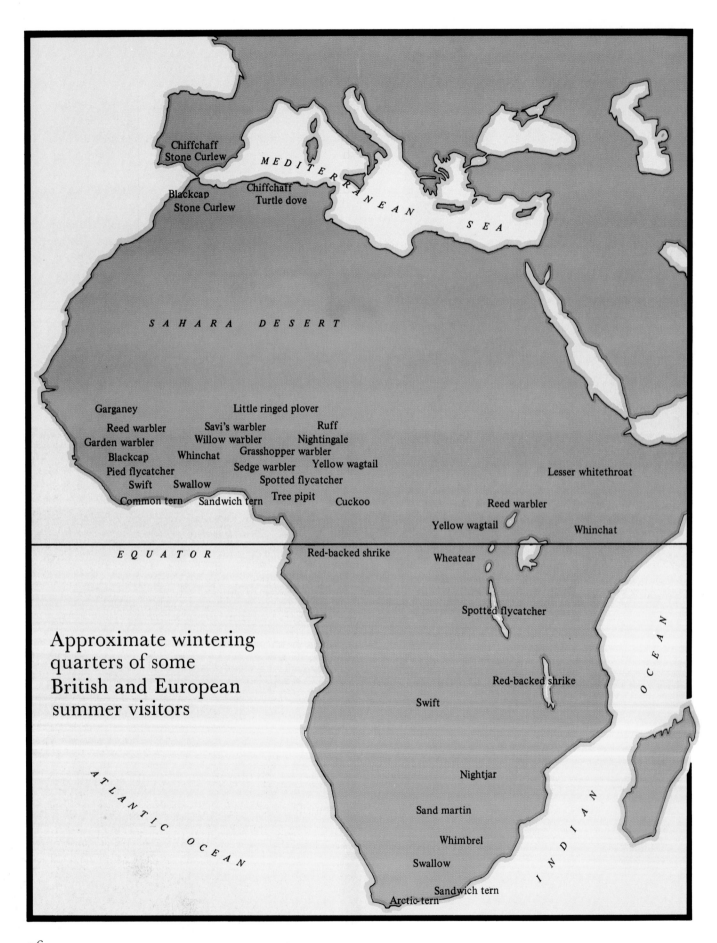

Chiffchaff
Stone Curlew

M E D I T E R R A N E A N

Blackcap
Stone Curlew

Chiffchaff
Turtle dove

S E A

S A H A R A   D E S E R T

Garganey   Little ringed plover
Reed warbler   Savi's warbler   Ruff
Garden warbler   Willow warbler   Nightingale
Blackcap   Whinchat   Grasshopper warbler
Pied flycatcher   Sedge warbler   Yellow wagtail
Swift   Swallow   Spotted flycatcher
Common tern   Sandwich tern   Tree pipit   Cuckoo   Lesser whitethroat

Reed warbler
Yellow wagtail
Whinchat

E Q U A T O R   Red-backed shrike   Wheatear

Spotted flycatcher

Red-backed shrike

Swift

A T L A N T I C   O C E A N

Approximate wintering quarters of some British and European summer visitors

Nightjar

Sand martin

Whimbrel

Swallow

Sandwich tern
Arctic tern

I N D I A N   O C E A N

marine vegetation on our coasts and estuaries. The Barnacle Goose, which prefers grass and is distinguished by its white face, also comes from the Arctic and winters mainly in the Hebrides, the Solway Firth and Ireland. Its curious name comes from the twelfth-century legend that the bird, whose nest nobody had seen, hatched from the shellfish (then called *bernaca*) which has a protuberance like a goose's neck. The *Oxford Dictionary*, however, says that the bird, not the crustacean, was first given that name.

The Wildfowl Trust, whose headquarters are at Slimbridge, Gloucestershire, organizes counts of all the swans, geese and ducks which winter with us and so is able to keep note of rises and falls in their numbers. Population changes can be caused by weather, persecution or protection by Man in their breeding areas and in their off-season feeding quarters where the amount of food also varies from winter to winter. Among the most common and widespread surface-feeding ducks, Mallard, Teal and Wigeon continue to keep good average numbers; some midwinter groups of each species in favourite sites reach many thousands.

ABOVE The small Barnacle Goose with its distinctive black neck and white face. It winters in the western Scottish isles and Ireland having bred in Greenland and Spitzbergen.

A colourful drake Wigeon preens itself. Small numbers of this species do breed in Britain, mostly in the north, but many thousands come as winter visitors or pause on their journey to Africa.

The Wood Sandpiper, a very few of which breed in central Scotland, is mostly seen as a passage migrant in spring and summer.

Shovelers, Gadwalls and Pintails are nowhere so numerous in the winter. The most common diving ducks, Pochard and Tufted, are increasing and the good numbers of these and the several other familiar waterfowl are due to a large extent to the work of our national and local conservation societies, good laws of protection and the efforts of the Wildfowlers' Association of Great Britain and Ireland, who do much to see that the laws are enforced and that birds are not over-shot.

Among the rarer species which might be spotted among our more common birds is the Ferruginous Duck, with much white on the wings like our other diving ducks but with a red body. It sometimes strays to our ponds and coastal waters from the southern half of Europe. The Marbled Teal and Red-crested Pochard, from the Mediterranean region, are also very rare; some which are seen might well have escaped from private collections, a possibility in the case of these and several other species which can have a bad effect on the records of the birdwatcher. The aptly named Long-tailed Duck, when seen, is more likely to be a genuinely wild bird. It has bred occasionally in Orkney and Shetland and occurs fairly often in the winter in these northern areas, much less so in southern England.

Of the visiting birds of prey, the Hen Harrier is the

most regular in more southerly, open areas away from its breeding range. Some sites, especially in the east and south, do not fail to have one or two from October to March. The Rough-legged Buzzard, from north Scandinavia and more easterly areas, is irregular but in some exceptional winters, as in 1974–5, four or five may spend the off-season together in one place, especially where Rabbits are numerous. In southern and eastern counties of England this buzzard may sometimes be seen being pursued by a Marsh Harrier whose territory it has invaded. Some of these open hunting areas are also used by single Great Grey Shrikes which prey upon small birds like Linnets, Twites, Stonechats and tits. The resident population of Merlins, which spreads out from breeding areas in the off-season, is added to by visitors from Iceland and northern Europe.

The numbers of our own Moorhens, Coots, Water Rails and Woodcock are also increased by birds from the Continent, but not very obviously so. Among the more noticeable additions to our native populations are the influxes of Lapwings, hundreds of thousands of which come across the North Sea between the first week of June and early winter and stay until spring. Equally early are the Curlews; these first migrants of autumn are probably failed breeders which have no need to stay longer in the north or east. They are soon followed by the young of those which were successful. Because the summers are short there, most waders which breed in the north leave as soon as they can. The Golden Plover is another such species and it soon appears in regular, favourite fields and stubbles in the south. Grey Plovers, identified in the off-season by their black under-arm patch and three-syllable whistle 'ee-eu-ee', which is like one human trying to attract the attention of another, are seen in much smaller groups on the shore and estuaries. They may be feeding in the same places as Oystercatchers, Curlews, Bar-tailed Godwits, Redshanks and Sanderlings, scattered over the mud and sand or along the edge of the tide.

Large, close-packed flocks of small, grey waders in such places below high-water mark are Dunlins and Knots, nervous and ready to take to the air to circle over the feeding area like fast-moving clouds of grey and white smoke. Many such groups, at any time between midsummer and early spring, will be birds on passage to more southerly areas; some will have been moved by bad weather from normally preferred feeding areas elsewhere.

More vegetated coastal areas of salt-marsh or wet, grassy places near by or inland are resorted to by an increasing number of Black-tailed Godwits in winter, especially in the east and south. Spotted Redshanks, now in their grey and white off-season plumage, also occur in these areas of fresh or saline water. Very few will remain throughout the winter

A Spotted Redshank in the grey and white plumage of winter. They nest in the north-west of Europe, their breeding plumage being mostly black with white spots on the upper parts. Small numbers winter in Britain but most go on to Africa.

Migrant Turnstones in winter plumage, which is far less colourful than their chestnut, black and white breeding dress. Many of them winter around British coasts, on both rocky and sandy shores.

Europe's smallest gull, the Little Gull, is seen mostly on passage in autumn. It is a northern species and one pair tried to breed in Britain in 1976, but unsuccessfully.

of the increasingly large number which would have been seen on passage since 12 June (the first birds of autumn are remarkably regular). Some Greenshanks may be seen in similarly varied feeding sites and at about the same times. On more rocky or stony coasts, as well as on sandy shores, Purple Sandpipers and Turnstones from Scandinavia and other northerly parts may be seen, most birds of the latter species being on passage and pausing to feed for only short periods.

Wintering on inland freshwater pools, old-fashioned sewage-works, water-cress beds and other shallow, well-vegetated wetlands, are unknown numbers of Jack Snipe. Their small size, $7\frac{1}{2}$ in. (190 mm), and brown and buff streaked plumage with purple and green gloss, make them difficult to see and they do not rise until they are almost trodden upon. A few Green Sandpipers, common as passage migrants in summer and autumn, may also overwinter in similar habitats, mainly in southern England.

Except for Kittiwakes, which will be at the coasts, and Lesser Black-backed Gulls, which are mainly summer visitors, common species of gulls will be found in a variety of places across the country in greater numbers in winter. On rare occasions, a Glaucous or an Iceland Gull may be seen, each identified from the other species as all-pale-grey birds with white wings (immatures are pale biscuit in colour). The Iceland Gull, the rarer of these two, breeds only in Greenland. It is smaller, more lightly built and has a shorter, thinner bill than the Glaucous. The comparatively tiny, 11-in. (280-mm) Little Gull, no bigger than a Common Tern and quite as graceful, is much more often seen especially on estuaries in south-east Scotland. Slightly larger and equally tern-like, Sabine's Gull, with its distinctive wing pattern of triangles of white, grey and black, and forked tail, is rare in winter, being a little more often seen when immatures on autumn passage pass down our coast from the Arctic.

Many thousands of Skylarks from central and northern Europe come into Britain every autumn. In midwinter they may be joined by many more, driven out of their normal wintering grounds, just across the North Sea, by snow and frost. These hard-weather movements occur down the whole of our east coast and often include refugees of many other species, like Shelduck, Brent Geese, Dunlins and Bramblings. The hardy birdwatcher has an exciting time on these occasions, if he can stand up to the rain, sleet or snow coming at him horizontally on strong, north-easterly winds, the conditions in which these movements most often take place. As soon as the weather improves he should watch again. The flocks being driven south a day or two before may now be hurrying back north. Many species dislike being displaced from their normal winter quarters.

A regular feeder on our east and south-east coasts, outside the breeding season, is the Shore Lark, distinctive with its black and yellow face and legs so bent it appears to shuffle among the salt-marsh vegetation, seaweed and stubbles in which it hunts for its food of seeds and invertebrates. With Shore Larks may be some Snow Buntings, recognized by their rusty-brown and white plumage and their butterfly appearance in flight. Their call is characteristic, a musical twitter being followed by a loud 'tsee-eu'. These last notes are very similar to those of the darker Lapland Bunting, a rare passage migrant, a few of which winter down our east coast. Rock Pipits from north-west Europe also use flat, coastal habitats in winter and are often seen in areas where the British populations do not breed. Water Pipits, a race of the same species which breeds in central and southern European mountains, are found on the coast and use inland, freshwater sites as well. They have paler upper parts and whiter under parts than the Rock Pipits and have bold, white eye stripes and much whiter outer tail feathers.

The Dunlin is one of the most common of Britain's migrant waders. Many breed in Britain, especially in the north, but very large flocks arrive from the Arctic Circle.

A Curlew Sandpiper, whose breeding range is in the high Arctic, pauses to feed on its return journey to tropical Africa. This bird still retains some of its colourful, red summer plumage and shows the down-curved bill which gives it its name.

The Little Stint, Europe's smallest wader, breeds in Siberia and migrates to southern Africa. Many pause *en route* to feed in Britain.

Other song birds which spend the off-season here, but in larger numbers, are Redwings and Fieldfares, both north-west European members of the thrush family which are beginning to colonize Britain in the north. The migrant flocks arrive in late September and in October when our hedgerows are full of berries, especially of hawthorn. When the most edible of these fruits have been eaten, the birds are more often seen feeding in fields. With them may be some of the several millions of Continental Starlings and, in stubbles and weedy areas, flocks of Chaffinches or Bramblings which move around according to the state of the weather and food availability.

The departure of all these birds begins as early as mid-February, if the weather is settled here and across the North Sea. According to the species and their destination, they will continue to depart until early May, and during this period they will be joined by passage migrants of the same or different species which have wintered farther south in Europe, or in Africa. The arrival of summer visitors soon adds to this traffic of millions of birds on the move at this vital period of the year.

First to return to their East Anglian breeding sites will probably be the hardy Avocets, soon to be followed by other waders and then by the huge variety of insect-eating song birds – warblers, flycatchers, martins and chats; the last to come being Swifts, Nightjars and Red-backed Shrikes.

The spring movement has hardly ceased when non-breeding or unsuccessful Lapwings and Curlews are seen on the move south or westwards again, often as early as 2 June. Hard on their heels comes a wide variety of other waders on their way from north-west Europe to winter quarters, many pausing for a few hours or a few days to feed and some to stay with us until next spring. Among the birds which will pass right through will be Curlew Sandpipers, like large Dunlins but with white rumps, paler upper parts and slightly more curved bill. Their numbers vary greatly each summer, as do those of the Little Stints, for they are affected by the amount of breeding success they have had in the Arctic and by the weather systems they meet on their southward flight. Spotted Redshanks – the first, early birds still wearing their dusky black plumage – Greenshanks, Common, Wood and Green Sandpipers, Ruffs, godwits of both species and Snipe will also be on the move early in summer and some of them will still be passing through in early October.

Small insect-eating birds start to leave us in early July and those from far afield in north-west Europe will begin to be seen in Britain in early August, especially when unfavourable winds and rain have caused them to lose their sense of direction on their night flight. Sometimes 'falls' of displaced night-migrants occur on our east coast, anywhere from Shetland to Kent, on a spectacular scale. The biggest arrival ever known occurred on 3 September 1965, when wet, easterly winds brought in millions of migrants of more than seventy species. In Suffolk, on the 18-mile (29-km) coastline from Minsmere to Lowestoft, between a quarter and half a million Redstarts fell out of the sky, as did tens of thousands of Wheatears, Pied and Spotted Flycatchers, Whitethroats, Willow and Garden Warblers and other small birds. There were also several Icterine Warblers and Wrynecks and unusually large numbers of other vagrants like Bluethroats, Barred Warblers and Ortolan Buntings which are normally seen only rarely.

Seed-eating birds like finches and buntings move mostly during October. They fly during the morning and feed in the afternoon when they come to suitable sites. They have a shorter migration to make than the insect-eaters, which have to fly by night on their way to Africa to give them time in the daylight to catch the large numbers of small invertebrates which they need. The exceptions are Swallows, martins and Swifts which migrate by day because they can catch their food as they go.

Starlings, Skylarks, Fieldfares, Redwings, Robins and crows are also mainly October arrivals from across the North Sea. They migrate by day or by night and the strength of their arrival is greatly affected by the weather. Persistent, strong north-west winds can force flocks southwards in Scandinavia to concentrate in Denmark or the Netherlands and to cross from there *en masse*. Sometimes Blackbirds, which do not normally fly in flocks, can arrive on the East Anglian coast by the thousand. Easterly winds in the autumn are the birdwatcher's delight – it's an ill wind for the birds that blows the birdwatcher good! From August to early November, onshore winds nearly always bring us some rarities blown off course from their southerly route towards Africa. As well as those unusual birds already mentioned, other vagrants which might with luck be found in our coastal bushes are Greenish, Arctic and Yellow-browed Warblers and Red-breasted Flycatchers. The rarest of all, Dusky, Radde's and Pallas's Warblers, may occur towards the end of the period, in late October or early November.

On the west side of Britain and Ireland, westerly winds bring a small, regular autumn crop of displaced waders, warblers, buntings and others from North America. They are first seen by birdwatchers who know when to organize their summer holidays in the Scillies and other good sites where these exhausted birds make their landfall. A good many birds, however, are able to spread themselves over the rest of the country in their search for food and at least one east-coast pool has had three different American waders feeding on its mud on the same day.

The Arctic Tern performs one of the most remarkable of bird migrations. It breeds mostly in the high Arctic and winters as far south as the coastline of the Antarctic.

103

6 Britain's Birdwatchers

The Chough, a member of Britain's family of crows, is distinctive in having a red, down-turned bill. It is not now common and nests in well-hidden caves and crannies in sea cliffs along the western coasts of the British Isles.

PREVIOUS PAGES A Little Grebe, the smallest member of Britain's grebe family, on the nest. It is widespread throughout Britain and in summer plumage can be identified by its reddish cheeks and upper neck. Its habitats are mainly reed and rush-grown lakes and quite small waters.

There are probably more birdwatchers to the square mile in Britain than in any other country. They are all kinds of people, young and old, academic and artisan, sociable and shy. In common, they all have a little or a lot of humanity and a certain amount of conscience about the state of the environment. Most are aware, some only vaguely, that Man depends upon the vitality of the wildlife around him and rightly they consider the existence of a good variety of birds as evidence of a reasonable balance in the ever-changing ecology.

The British public enjoys excellent and frequent nature programmes on television and radio. These, all the many fine bird books, and the rest of the media keep us aware of the worsening quality of our habitat and other misfortunes of modern living and are gently instructive about conservation. As a nation of animal-lovers we are not merely passive. The variety of organizations we have set up is actively concerned about the welfare of a wide range of wildlife and is increasingly influencing the thinking of the Government and other users of land and water. Those of our fifty-six million population who are energetically conservation-minded are relatively few, but their number is growing rapidly.

Most people who subscribe to a wildlife protection society support one mainly concerned with birds, partly, perhaps, in envy or admiration of them because they are what the world now allows so few of us to be – as free as a bird. Membership of the Royal Society for the Protection of Birds and its Young Ornithologists' Club has leapt from six thousand to 325,000 in the past quarter-century, which may suggest a preference for birds at the expense of other wild animals and plants but this is not so. A very large part of the revenue of the RSPB and other bodies goes into getting hold of all the wilderness land it can, and the societies managing the habitat mainly for the birds there take better-than-ever care of all other species of its fauna and flora. Wild land of little or no agricultural value is not often on the market, however, and it is increasingly expensive. To avoid covering still more good growing soil with houses and industrial development, heaths are being cleared and wetlands drained. The total amount of land which the national and local conservation bodies have been able to acquire and manage for wildlife still amounts to no more than one per cent of Britain's surface.

Some people go out to watch birds because of their beauty, with no conscious intention of escaping for a while from the pace of an overcrowded, technological, disciplined life. Many, however, do realize the good effect on our health of being absorbed in watching the uninhibited behaviour of wild things, especially birds which are beautiful, extremely agile and more than a little mysterious, and these

people get great value from regular visits to good places. Doctors prescribe this form of unwinding and many practise what they preach. There is no need to go far. Intrepid tits, watchful thrushes and a Robin 'holding' the area can be attracted to feed outside the window and often within. A Kestrel can be seen hovering over the city and can give pleasure in the thought that our once-callous attitude towards wild creatures has so improved in this century that wherever it nests on a building it will be welcomed. The ducks winging over Hyde Park in the winter and the Black-headed Gulls which one person, at least, has had time to stop and feed during the rush hour ant-procession over London Bridge, can be imagined as having come from Arctic Russia, as well they might, or from just down the river on the Essex or Kent marshes.

Birdwatching, a pursuit which still raised eyebrows in the 1930s, is now well accepted. Once done almost exclusively by the middle classes alone – several ornithological works of

The Black-winged Stilt is a vagrant wader which did once nest in Britain, near Nottingham in 1945 when the three pairs raised three young. They can now, although rarely, be seen by keen birdwatchers in south-east England in spring and autumn but no attempts have been made by them to breed in Britain since 1945.

107

Part of a large flock of several thousand Oystercatchers roosting while their feeding area, the mud flats of the Cheshire Dee estuary, is under high tide. These birds breed throughout Britain and are joined by many thousands of migrants from more northerly countries.

the eighteenth and nineteenth centuries were by doctors, headmasters, parsons and others with time to spare – it is now a fast-growing leisure industry and, like angling, our most popular participation sport, it is highly democratic. National bodies like the RSPB, the Nature Conservancy Council, the Scottish Wildlife Trust, the Council for the Protection of Rural Wales and the many county Naturalists' Trusts have bird reserves scattered across Britain where people of all kinds meet and discuss their hobby. Her Majesty the Queen is patron of the RSPB and the Duke of Edinburgh is also a keen and very experienced birdwatcher. Above all, birdwatching is or should be the most relaxed and relaxing of hobbies. Perhaps the only custom among birdwatchers is that the wearing of old, comfortable clothes is expected. Expertise is not looked for and if you started today much friendly help would be available if you wanted it.

A birdwatcher can be one of a party or a pair, or can keep his or her own company. On a reserve, in one of the big, permanent hides, you can join in any discussion or can remain quiet and listen, to learn from others or to practise birdmanship, the art of letting others do the guessing about a bird's identity or the reasons for an aspect of its behaviour. To be a birdwatcher you do not need to spend much money. Binoculars, which need cost only a few pounds, are the most expensive item and a good field bird identification guide is also necessary.

Membership of a national or local society, preferably both, is advisable in order to be kept in the picture and is a splendid way of making friends. Travel is a matter of ambition; for some, it is a lucky posting in one of HM Forces, each of which has its own Ornithological Society, notably the RAFOS, which plays an important part in aircraft safety.

A person who gets pleasure from watching birds is likely to be one who respects the countryside and knows that since almost all of the land is privately owned he may not go everywhere he pleases, though there is considerable freedom in open country in Scotland. But, as in all other pursuits with scope for one-upmanship, birdwatching can bring out the less courteous side of the nature of a minority. When a man, substituting a fierce hunting instinct with ornithology, has become obsessed with the desire to collect a long list of bird species he has seen, a good enough ambition in itself, he may well openly trespass in order to see the latest wind-blown stray. For a while among the young, more desperate hunters there was a cult of 'trespass until caught rules OK' and when intercepted you simply went quietly away. But such behaviour was not really practicable and led to defensive action by unfortunate owners of land at the coast where rare birds more often appeared; most keen list-keepers have come to realize that the best chance of seeing a rarity is to ask permission. If the rare bird is on a reserve with facilities for visitors, there is little problem. British birdwatching hides, still of the design invented by the RSPB in 1947, with covered approaches, viewing slots, seats and arm-rests, are the best there are for public use and do not deter birds from coming very close to the observers within, even though they may all be talking excitedly together; it is appearance and movement that mostly frightens birds away.

The really desperate pursuer of records often makes a long journey to a remote place when the highly efficient network of hot-lines informs him of the latest arrival; he is not put off by the fact that the bird might well have moved on by the time he gets there. Such people are called 'twitchers' or 'tickers', and a new bird ticked off on a life list is a 'tick' or a 'lifer'. Curiously enough, although there are as many women birdwatchers as there are men, few get the rare-bird bug. A small number, deserted at week-ends by their husbands or boyfriends who have gone off on what is often a wild goose chase, dislike the hobby. Many women, on the other hand, have become birdwatchers because they were golf widows. Apart from any very occasional bad effect on human relationships, rare-bird hunting is a harmless obsession, not contributing a great deal to ornithology although the detailed descriptions, photographs and,

A Selection of Bird Reserves,
Wildfowl Refuges and
Migration Observation Stations
in the British Isles

1 Herma Ness NNR
2 Fetlar RSPB
3 Noss NNR
4 Fair Isle NTS
5 Noup Cliffs RSPB
6 Marwick Head RSPB
7 Hobbister RSPB
8 Hoy (Private)
9 Copinsay RSPB
10 Munlochy Bay R & CCC
11 Loch of Strathbeg RSPB
12 Loch Garten RSPB
13 Insh Marshes RSPB
14 Cairngorms NNR
15 Sands of Forvie NNR
16 Fowlsheugh RSPB
17 Loch of Lowes SWT
18 Loch Leven NNR
19 Vane Farm RSPB
20 Isle of May NNR
21 Aberlady Bay LNR/ELCC
22 Bass Rock (Private)
23 Holy Island NNR
24 Farne Islands NT
25 Washington WT
26 Cowpen Marsh RSPB
27 Bempton Cliffs RSPB
28 Hornsea Mere RSPB
29 Fairburn Ings RSPB
30 Blacktoft Sands RSPB
31 Spurn Head YNT
32 Tetney Marshes RSPB
33 Gibraltar Point LNR
34 Attenborough LNR
35 Empingham Reservoir
AWA

36 Peakirk WT
37 Grafham Water AWA
38 Wicken Fen NT
39 Ouse Washes RSPB
40 Welney WT
41 Snettisham RSPB
42 Holme NNT
43 Titchwell RSPB
44 Scolt Head NNR
45 Holkham NNR
46 Blakeney Point NT
47 Cley Marshes NNT/NT
48 Horsey Mere NT
49 Hickling NNR
50 Breydon Water LNR
51 Oulton Broad
52 Walberswick NNR
53 Minsmere RSPB
54 Havergate Island RSPB
55 The Lodge & Sutton Fen RSPB
56 Tring Reservoir NNR
57 Rye House Marsh RSPB
58 Abberton Reservoir AWA
59 Fingringhoe Wick ENT
60 Epping Forest
61 Brent Reservoir
62 Barn Elms Reservoir
63 Northward Hill RSPB
64 Elmley Marshes RSPB
65 Bough Beech KNT/SWA
66 Stodmarsh NNR
67 Sandwich Bay KNT/NT
68 Dungeness RSPB
69 Rye Harbour LNR
70 Seven Sisters and Cuckmere Haven ESCC
71 Arundel WT
72 Pagham Harbour LNR
73 Chichester Harbour
74 Newtown Harbour LNR
75 Stanpit Marshes LNR
76 Brownsea Island NT/DNT
77 Arne RSPB
78 Radipole Lake RSPB
79 Portland Bill

80 Abbotsbury Swannery (Private)
81 Exe Estuary NWR
82 Slapton Ley FSC
83 Tamar Estuary CNT
84 St Agnes (Private)
85 Lundy NT
86 Chapel Wood RSPB
87 Slimbridge WT
88 Nags Head RSPB
89 Oxwich NNR
90 Skokholm Island FSC
91 Skomer NNR
92 Grassholm RSPB
93 Ramsey (Private)
94 Gwenffwd/Dinas RSPB
95 Ynys-hir RSPB
96 Lake Vyrnwy RSPB
97 Coombes Valley RSPB
98 Bardsey LNR
99 Newborough Warren NNR
100 South Stack Cliffs RSPB
101 Hilbre Island (Private)
102 Martin Mere WT
103 Wyre/Lune NWR
104 Leighton Moss and Morecambe Bay RSPB
105 Calf of Man MM/NT
106 Langness MM/NT
107 Ravenglass CCC
108 St Bees Head RSPB
109 Caerlaverock NNR
110 Mull of Galloway RSPB
111 Lochwinnoch RSPB
112 Loch Lomond NNR
113 Rhum NNR
114 Benn Eighe NNR
115 St Kilda NTS/NCC
116 Balranald RSPB
117 Handa Island RSPB
118 Rathlin Island Cliffs RSPB
119 Shanes Castle RSPB
120 Castle Caldwell RSPB
121 Saltee Island (Private)
122 Cape Clear (Private)

AWA Anglian Water Authority
CCC Cumbria County Council
CNT Cornwall Naturalists' Trust
DNT Dorset Naturalists' Trust
ELCC East Lothian County Council
ENT Essex Naturalists' Trust
ESCC East Sussex County Council
FSC Field Studies Council
KNT Kent Naturalists' Trust
LNR Local Nature Reserve (Society for the Promotion of Nature Conservancy and the County Naturalists' Trust)
MM Manx Museum
NNR National Nature Reserve (Nature Conservancy Council)
NT National Trust
NTS National Trust for Scotland
R & CCC Ross and Cromarty County Council
RSPB Royal Society for the Protection of Birds
SWA Southern Water Authority
SWT Scottish Wildlife Trust
WT Wildfowl Trust
YNT Yorkshire Naturalists' Trust

sometimes, tape-recordings which occasionally result are valuable. It is better than the old method of accepting only the evidence of the bird's dead body. In a time not so very long ago when we had little or no feeling for wild things and high-powered optical equipment was not so readily available while guns were, a philosophy of 'What's hit's history, what's missed is mystery' was perhaps understandable.

It is less than half a century since egg-collecting by boys (almost never by girls) ceased to be one of the accepted seasonal hobbies, to give way to cricket and swimming as spring gave way to summer. Now oology, as it is known, is unpopular and all wild birds' eggs are protected by law, forcing the professional collector or dealer to take part in a high-priced underground market. At school, the swapping of blown eggs has been replaced by joining the bird club organized by a keen and knowledgeable teacher who takes his or her boys and girls on field trips. Many make up working-parties on nearby bird reserves, clearing scrub and ditches and assisting in other management tasks. Modern methods of active conservation, which are taking over from the type of preservation where Man does not interfere and where aggressive action is advisable in the long term, call for a great deal of such free organized gang-labour. The workers are given splendid facilities for observing birds and learning about their needs and they are further rewarded with a sense of fulfilment in having helped nature, human society and themselves.

Young people may encourage their parents to take up birdwatching or the interest may have been instilled by one or both adults. Complete family parties, sharing a healthy mutual interest – and sharing binoculars and the cost of transport – are frequently to be seen at good places at weekends and holidays. Like the parents, all the conservation organizations encourage young naturalists because it is they who will have the task of caring for the shrinking environment of the future which is at present under attack. There is little difficulty in filling vacancies or finding trainees for new conservation posts as they arise. Many young people are prepared to suffer in order to get a foot in the conservation world, accepting part-time employment, minimum wages, working for nothing during vacations, cheerfully putting up with primitive living conditions and doing the most menial jobs. For several years they will not mind having a humble position. Prince Philip once said that a man should not be judged by his position or wealth but by how well he serves society in whatever high or low capacity. Similarly, history may not decide how civilized a nation has become by the size of its armed forces or what its industry produces but by how well it cared for its own section of the world environment.

British Conservation Organizations

Some of the organizations concerned with the welfare of birds in the British Isles are:

Army Bird Watching Society, c/o Army Apprentices College, Harrogate, Yorks.

Association for the Protection of Rural Scotland, 20 Falkland Avenue, Newton, Nairn, Renfrewshire, G77 5DR.

British Naturalists' Association, Willowfield, Boyneswood Road, Four Marks, Alton, Hants.

British Ornithologists' Union, c/o The Zoological Society, Regent's Park, London, NW1 4RY.

British Trust for Ornithology, Beech Grove, Tring, Herts, HP23 5NR.

Council for Nature, c/o The Zoological Society, Regent's Park, London, NW1 4RY.

Council for the Preservation of Rural England, 4 Hobart Place, London, SW1.

Council for the Preservation of Rural Wales, 14 Broad Street, Welshpool, Powys, SY21 7SD.

Countryside Commission, John Dower House, Crescent Place, Cheltenham, Gloucestershire, GL50 3RA.

Countryside Commission for Scotland, Battleby, Redgorton, Perth, PH1 3EW.

Countryside Commission, Committee for Wales, 8 Broad Street, Newton, Powys, Wales.

Fauna Preservation Society, c/o Zoological Society, Regent's Park, London, NW1 4RY.

Field Studies Council, 9 Devereux Court, London, WC2.

Forestry Commission, 231 Corstorphine Road, Edinburgh, EH12 7AT.

International Council for Bird Preservation, c/o British Museum (Natural History), Cromwell Road, London, SW7 5BD.

Irish Wildbird Conservancy, c/o Royal Irish Academy, 19 Dawson Street, Dublin, 2.

London Natural History Society, 142 Harborough Road, London, SW16.

Manx National Trust, Manx Museum, Douglas, Isle of Man.

National Parks Commission, 1 Cambridge Gate, London, NW1.

National Trust, 42 Queen Anne's Gate, London, SW1.

National Trust for Scotland, 5 Charlotte Square, Edinburgh, EH2 4DU.

Nature Conservancy Council, 19 Belgrave Square, London, SW1.

Royal Air Force Ornithological Society, HQ Training Command, RAF Brampton, Huntingdonshire, PE18 8QL.

Royal Naval Bird Watching Society, 23 St David's Road, Southsea, Hants.

Royal Society for the Prevention of Cruelty to Animals, Causeway, Horsham, Sussex, RH12 1HG.

Royal Society for the Protection of Birds, The Lodge, Sandy, Beds, SG19 2DL.

Scottish Field Studies Association, 141 Bath Street, Glasgow.

Scottish Ornithologists' Club, 21 Regent Terrace, Edinburgh, EH7 5BN.

Scottish Wildlife Trust, 8 Dublin Street, Edinburgh, EH1 3PP.

Seabird Group, c/o British Ornithologists' Union, Zoological Society, Regent's Park, London, NW1 4RY.

Selborne Society, 57 Corfton Road, London, W5.

Society for the Promotion of Nature Conservation, The Green, Nettleham, Lincoln, LN2 2NR.

Wildfowl Trust, Slimbridge, Gloucestershire.

Wildfowlers' Association of Great Britain and Ireland, Marford Mill, Rossett, Clwyd, LL12 0HL.

World Wildlife Fund, 29 Greville Street, London, EC1N 8AX.

Young Ornithologists' Club, Royal Society for the Protection of Birds, The Lodge, Sandy, Beds, SG19 2DL.

Zoological Society of London, Regent's Park, London, NW1 4RY.

Bibliography and Further Reading

Axell, H., and Hosking, E., *Minsmere: Portrait of a Bird Reserve* (Hutchinson, London 1977)

Bannerman, D.A., *The Birds of the British Isles*, 12 vols (Oliver & Boyd, London and Edinburgh, 1953–63)

British Ornithologists' Union, *The Status of Birds in Britain and Ireland* (Blackwell, Edinburgh and Oxford, 1971)

British Trust for Ornithology and Irish Wildbird Conservancy, comp. J.T.R. Sharrock, *The Atlas of Breeding Birds in Britain and Ireland* (BTO, Tring, 1976)

Brown, L., *British Birds of Prey* (Collins, London, 1976)

Brown, P., and Waterston, G., *The Return of the Osprey* (Collins, London, 1962)

Campbell, B., *The Oxford Book of Birds* (Oxford University Press, London, 1964)

Cramp, S., Bourne, W.R.P., and Saunders, D., *The Sea Birds of Britain and Ireland* (Collins, London, 1974)

Duffey, E. *Nature Reserves and Wildlife* (Heinemann, London, 1974)

Fitter, R.S.R., *Collins Guide to Bird Watching* (Collins, London, 1963)

Gooders, J., *Where to Watch Birds in Britain and Europe* (Andre Deutsch, London, 1970)

Heinzel, H., Fitter, R., and Parslow, J., *The Birds of Britain and Europe* (Collins, London, 1972)

Hollom, P.A.D., *The Popular Handbook of British Birds* (Witherby, London, 1962)

Lack, D., *Enjoying Ornithology* (Methuen, London, 1965)

Lack, D., *Population Studies of Birds* (Clarendon Press, Oxford, 1966)

Macleod, R.D., *Key to the Names of British Birds* (Pitman, London, 1954)

Murton, R.K., *Man and Birds* (Collins, London, 1971)

Parslow, J., *Breeding Birds of Britain and Ireland* (Poyser, London, 1973)

Peterson, R., Mountfort, G., and Hollom, P.A.D., *Birds of Britain and Europe* (Collins, London, 1966)

Reade, W., and Hosking, E., *Nesting Birds, Eggs and Fledglings* (Blandford, London, 1967)

Sheail, J., *Nature in Trust* (Blackie, Glasgow and London, 1976)

Simms, E., *Woodland Birds* (Collins, London, 1971)

Thompson, A.L. (ed.), *A New Dictionary of Birds* (Nelson, London and Edinburgh, 1964)

Witherby, H.F., Jourdain, F.C.R., Ticehurst, N.F., and Tucker, B.W., *The Handbook of British Birds*, 5 vols (Witherby, London, 1949)

Yapp, W.B., *Birds and Woods* (Oxford University Press, London, 1962)

Yarrell, W., *A History of British Birds*, 3 vols (Van Voorst, London, 1843)

Index

Page numbers in italic refer to the illustrations